# BEHAVE YOURSELF!

Straight Talk, Common Sense and Encouragement of

Nick Seta

Edited by
Lynn Seta

Cedar River Publishing

Cincinnati, Ohio

Behave Yourself!
Straight Talk, Common Sense and Encouragement of Nick Seta

Edited by
Lynn Seta

ISBN 978-1-7320627-9-5

Copyright © 2024 by Lynn Seta.
All rights reserved. No part of this book may be reproduced, transmitted, or stored in an information retrieval system in any form or by any means, graphic, electronic, or mechanical, including photocopying, taping, and recording, without prior written permission from the author. For permission requests solicit the author via www.lynnseta.com

Creative Direction and Editing by Jennifer Holder
Interior Setup and Design - Franklin Seta
Cover Design by Knoll Gilbert
Printed in the United States of America

Scripture quotations marked NIV are taken from the Holy Bible, New International Version*, NIV© 1973, 1978, 1984, 2011 by Biblica, Inc. Used with permission from Zondervan. All rights reserved worldwide. (www.zondervan.com)

The "NIV" and the "New International Version" are trademarks registered in the United States Patent and Trademark Office by Biblica, Inc.

# Table of Contents

**Preface and Dedication** ...................................................................... 7
**The Beginning** ......................................................................................... 9
**The Talks** ................................................................................................. 21
**Common Sense about Kids**
Talk #1 The Ten Commandments of Surface Behavior ....................... 25
Talk #2 Become A Master Artist: The Fine Art of Molding Human Behavior ...................................................................................................... 31
Talk #3 Causes or Changes: Two Approaches to Analysis ................. 35
Talk #4 Discipline for Teens ..................................................................... 39
Talk #5 Solving the Puzzle of Failing Children ..................................... 43
Talk #6 Differences in Difficult Kids ...................................................... 45
**Common Sense about Leadership**
Talk #7 Leadership Point of View ........................................................... 53
Talk #8 Listen to Them .............................................................................. 59
Talk #9 How to Become an Effective, Aggressive Listener ................ 65
Talk #10 The Productive Personality ...................................................... 71
Talk #11 Motivation ................................................................................... 73
Talk #12 Obligations of Managers and Supervisors ............................. 79
Talk #13 Two Common Difficulties Leaders Face ................................ 83
Talk #14 Stress the Destroyer ................................................................... 87
**Common Sense about Christian Life**
Talk #15 The Responsible Christian ........................................................ 91
Talk #16 Christians as Role Models, Christian Obedience ................. 95
Talk #17 Do Not Judge .............................................................................. 99
Talk #18 Be Patient .................................................................................. 101
**The Ending** ............................................................................................ 103
**Knowing Nick: Memories and Photos**
Reflections From Friends and Family .................................................. 104
Transcript of Columbus Day Dinner Speech at the Sons of Italy ..... 113
Photos from Nick's History .................................................................... 120
Nick in the News ...................................................................................... 137
Nick's Expose on Gambling ................................................................... 166

# Preface and Dedication

*"When the sun goes below the horizon, he is not set; the heavens glow for a full hour after his departure. And when a great and good man sets, the sky of this world is luminous long after he is out of sight. Such a man cannot die out of this world. When he goes, he leaves behind him much of himself. Being dead, he speaks."*
–Henry Ward Beecher

When Victor Hugo was past eighty years of age, he gave expression to his religious faith in these sublime sentences:

*"I feel in myself the future life. I am like a forest that has been more than once cut down. The new shoots are livelier than ever. I am rising toward the sky. The sunshine is on my head. The earth gives me its generous sap, but heaven lights me with its unknown worlds."*

*"You say the soul is nothing but the resultant of the bodily powers. Why, then, is my soul more luminous when my bodily powers begin to fail? Winter is on my head, but eternal spring is in my heart. I breathe at this hour the fragrance of the lilacs, the violets, and the roses as at twenty years. The nearer I approach the end, the plainer I hear around me the immortal symphonies of the worlds which invite me. It is marvelous, yet simple."*

Nick Seta passed from this life at age ninety. Five days before his death, he requested that his family gather in his room.

We were his last and best speaking engagement. Though his voice was weak, it still was easily heard by all. His words to us were filled with encouragement, some laughs, and of course, tears. With love, this book is dedicated to his nine children, thirteen grandchildren, five great-grandchildren, and all who come after them.

–L.S.

## The Beginning

In this age of Ancestry.com, many of us take the test to find out "our roots." One of Nick Seta's daughters did just that. And, to no one's surprise, Ancestery.com reported she is 50% from Calabria, a warm, picturesque region in the south of Italy. This is where the story of Nicholas Andrew Seta begins. He always claimed to be "One Hundred Percent Italian." In fact, Nick liked to say the blood of Caesars ran through his veins. He certainly looked it. At five feet, seven inches on a tall day, with olive skin, black hair and piercing dark eyes, he was definitely Caesar . . . or perhaps Godfather material; quite handsome, in my opinion.

Nick was born in the mountain town of Fuscaldo. As you might expect in a mountain town, Fuscaldo had narrow roads, scary, winding, switchback trails, similar to our roads deep in the Appalachian Mountains. That is where any resemblance to America ended. This town was built centuries ago, and many of the homes are built on the solid rock of the mountain. Almost every house has a view. They all look out over the landscape, down to the sea on one side and the other next to a street. Besides the narrow roadways, there were steps throughout the town. Should the streets be cut off, you could get from the top of the town to the convent at the bottom by these steps.

Along with the convent, Fuscaldo has at least seven Catholic churches; old, sacred and beautiful. Halfway up the mountain is the piazza, where people meet to share the day's happenings, have a glass of Strega and listen to Nick's grandfather's poems, speeches and wise wisdom. If you keep walking to the top you can see the remains of Duke Spinelli's castle. Doesn't it sound romantic, idyllic?

Nick's parents, Maria and Francesco, were also born in Fuscaldo and lived there most of their lives. I was blessed to visit this place three times. It was perfect; with window boxes of flowers, laundry on the line and the aromas of delicious food cooking. The house is still there as well as the bed in which Nick was born. On my first visit, I slept in that very bed and I walked the stone steps Nick's little feet had once trod.

By the 1920s, many southern Italians, including some Seta relatives, had already immigrated to America. When a tragedy came to Maria and Francesco's home, the family also decided to immigrate. They had lost their little five-year-old daughter Melina to diphtheria. Though their son was also ill, he survived. With the heartbreak of grief and the poor economic climate of southern Italy, Maria and Francesco applied for papers to travel to a new beginning in the land of opportunity. Frank left first. Maria, little Nicky and others from Fuscaldo followed in 1927, traveling to Napoli where they boarded the boat to America.

Nicky was almost two and a smart, precocious little guy. Being in cramped living quarters as they sailed across the ocean was challenging. Among the many incidents that made the crossing memorable was the day Little Nicky disappeared—a horror no mother would want to experience. Maria was frantic. When she and the others from Fuscaldo realized he was missing, they searched and searched, shouting for him and crying many fearful tears. When the search was expanded to the next deck, one flight above, they found a crowd of people, clapping and singing. Here they found Nicky in the middle of them all, dancing while the music played and collecting coins that were tossed at his feet.

As most Italian immigrants did, Maria and Nicky arrived at Ellis Island and were welcomed by Lady Liberty on October 11, 1927, though New York wasn't the final destination for the

Fuscaldese..

The Frank Seta family and many others from their small town settled in the tenements on Main Street in downtown Cincinnati, Ohio. Nick's father had a barber shop at 1310 Main Street, and Maria worked at the tailor shop as a finisher of custom-made suits. Nicky went to daycare at St. Mary's Institute. Many of the old Cincinnati buildings remain to this day, so when, many years later, Nick walked Main Street, he walked it with so many memories keeping him company.

I would like to pause and reflect on the immigration of this family. I have great respect for what they did. Leaving family members behind and the only home they had ever known was so brave. The task of working through governmental requirements and boarding a ship bound for a new place where they didn't know the language and were alone must have taken such mettle. I am in awe! Many Italians who came to Cincinnati in those days opened businesses and became successful, even millionaires. Nick's mom and dad worked hard, saved money, sent money home to their relatives in Fuscaldo, and lived in the land of freedom and hope.

Nick, his cousins and friends grew up and roamed the streets of Cincinnati in the 1930s. He and his cousins became partners in crime. Carlo and Bill figured out a way to get into the Blue Bird Bakery and get a pie. Since Nicky was the smallest, Carlo and Bill hoisted him up through the transom at the top of the door. Then down went Nick to let Carlo and Bill in for dessert. Along with finding a way to get a pie, they also managed to steal into the movies occasionally by distraction and other devious measures.

As adventuresome as he was together with his cousins, young Nicky also managed to have escapades on his own. Woolworths seemed to hold a fascination for him. Once, while still in knickers, this little Italian boy cut out the pockets of those same knickers and went shopping. That is to say, he filled his pockets with handfuls of marbles. Spotted by the store clerk, Nicky took off running but soon was apprehended and taken to his father's barbershop. While a very fast runner, it seems Nicky had not calculated the weight of the marbles filling his knickers, which slowed him down.

Another story that found him at Woolworths was when little Nicky wanted a goldfish for a pet. Woolworths had aquariums filled with goldfish in the back of the store, and after just a few tries, he caught a goldfish with his hand. Out to the sidewalk he ran, spitting in the face of the fish. While home was close, the fish didn't make it.

There are many other stories like these about Nick's early years. Some were funny, and others were highly challenging for his parents. It did seem running was always a part of the story: run to school so the bigger boys wouldn't steal his lunch; run home from the grocery with the food his mom had requested; run away, after the gang from a few streets over decided to fight with Nicky and his friends and the cops were on their way!

The last story I'll share is one Nick's mother shared with me. It is priceless, poor Mama! Nick decided he wanted a kitty, and it happened that the neighbor had quite a few of them. Nicky brought all of the kittens home and hid them under his bed. The neighborhood policeman soon knocked on the Setas' door with a complaint. While Maria, who did not yet speak English very well, insisted, "No, no, no cats here," four little purebred Persian kittens came walking into the room. Nicky was the only surviving child of Maria and Frank Seta, but that day was a close call for him! Nick was their joy and frustration.

Besides being at daycare at St. Mary's, Nick attended St. Mary's (all boys) elementary school and was an altar boy at St. Mary's Church. He learned to read and write English early, which became a blessing to all of the aunts, uncles, and cousins who would gather at night to listen to Nicky. Around age ten, he began reading the accounts of Benito Mussolini's rise to power and all the other news about Poland, France, Germany, and Great Britain leading up to the war in Europe.

Nick kept reading the newspaper all his life, feeling it was best to be in touch with the climate of his community and the world. He encouraged others to do the same.

While Nick enjoyed reading the newspaper to his relatives, he began developing another ability that would pay his way through college. By age fourteen, Nick was adept at dealing cards and taught himself to cheat with that same deck. While attending Purcell High School, an all-boys school at that time, Nick also dealt across the river in the clubs of Newport. His Uncle Tony introduced him to the owners, and Nick had a job. He told his mom and dad he delivered newspapers, and they were proud of their son. He kept his real job a secret. At a time when it was needed, he was able to contribute generously to the family's finances.

During high school, Nick and his family lived at the corner of Dorchester and Young. Assigned to trim the bushes, he became so focused on perfecting his job that the bushes were almost to the ground when he finished. Needless to say, his father was not a happy man. Nick realized he had done well; as now his dad would no longer ask him to do bush trimming. Since trimming bushes was not where his skills and abilities lay, anyway. He continued to deal cards across the river. He was an excellent student and enjoyed track, boxing, football and baseball. While enjoying neighborhood groups that played all sorts of games on the streets, Nick went to pool halls, where he became proficient with a cue stick.

He graduated from Purcell High School in June 1943. I'm sure it was difficult for his parents when Nick finally told his mom and dad he wanted to join in the fight for his country. On February 21, 1944, his dad walked with him to the recruiting station and Nick enlisted in the Marines.

Nick left Union Terminal headed for the west coast. After training, he arrived in the Pacific Arena on April 2, 1945. He fought in Saipan, The Marshalls, Okinawa, and five other islands. Like many men shipped to the South Pacific, his family realized they wouldn't know where he was so before leaving the US, Nick and his parents worked out a code so that when he sent correspondence they could tell where he was when he wrote it.

During World War II the Marine Corps and fighting in the islands profoundly impacted Nick's life. You've probably heard the saying, "Once a Marine, always a Marine." That was undoubtedly true of Nick Seta. Now we have an Italian American Marine. Wow! During his time in the Marines, his skill at cards became a vital pastime and money-maker. Nick would say he didn't cheat his Marine buddies, only the Navy guys. Sgt. Nicholas Seta returned to American soil on May 25, 1946, and was discharged from the Marine Corps on June 8, 1946, MCAS, Miramar, San Diego, California.

He enjoyed west coast gambling, and eventually, his life touched the professional gambling world. But Nick couldn't stay there, and he found his way back to Cincinnati and enrolled in Xavier University, graduating with his bachelor's in June 1951.

Gambling did play an essential role in his later success by becoming a vehicle for educating the public regarding the dangers of gambling and its addiction. His famous card shows would later bring in funds for the children under his care.

Like many WW II Veterans, Nick came home and settled in Cincinnati near his mom and dad. While attending college, he worked several jobs, including one for the USPS. He also continued to utilize his card skills by dealing at the clubs in Newport, Kentucky.

When he graduated from Xavier, he was hired by Cincinnati Public Schools and found that he truly enjoyed teaching the boys in his class. In a nutshell, he was good at it! His charm, innate common sense, wisdom and experiences as a street kid helped him relate to children in need. During this time, he also did card shows for clubs and men's groups. Little did he know his life was about to change when, at one such show in downtown Cincinnati, there was an astute gentleman who was looking for a man just like Nick. His name was Dr. Goldman. At the time, he was the superintendent of Longview State Hospital, located on the city's outskirts.

Dr. Goldman approached Nick and explained that the hospital was receiving more children who needed their own space and programs instead of being housed with the adults. This was the beginning of the Children's Unit School and a life-changing move for Nick. He became the director and also the principal of the school. It was a residential treatment center for emotionally disturbed children and children with psychiatric illnesses such as schizophrenia.

Nick liked to say when Dr. Goldman first approached him, he didn't know how to spell psychiatric. The Children's Unit School of Longview State Hospital was the first educational and recreational program in America for mentally ill and severely emotionally disturbed children housed in a state mental institution.

It was the early 50's, and Nick was given an old TB ward at the hospital for the school. In the ensuing years, he turned the space into classrooms for art, home economics class, and an industrial arts shop. He also created offices for the administration including social workers, two psychiatrists', and a dentist. On the lower level he made a recreational hall and cafeteria and a few years later he built a basketball court and a parking lot too. Eventually he was successful in raising enough money to purchase vans to take the children on educational field trips to parks and special events throughout the year.

Nick believed healing and helping children to integrate back into society required everyday activities, a continuing education, and a sense of accomplishment and belonging. If the child was capable, he or she was given a task (work) to do with a reward for a job well done. They had recreation after school, staffed by college students, employees and volunteers. Nick conducted tours of the Children's Unit School and spoke to many groups about the school's needs. The vans, Home Economics, Art and Industrial Arts teachers were, to a great extent, furnished by the community.

Nick ran the Children's Unit School and later the new facilities of Millcreek Children's Psychiatric Center from 1951 until 1979. Being full of energy, he did several other jobs during this period of time. From 1955 until 1979 Nick also ran a school at the Hamilton County Juvenile Court Center located at 2020 Auburn Avenue and worked under Judge Benjamin Schwartz and Judge David Grossman.

He finished his Master's Degree at Xavier University in 1957 and, in 1958, began as an associate professor at the university, developing classes to train workers to meet the needs of mentally ill and severely disturbed children. His Saturday classes of "Introduction to the Emotionally Disturbed Child," "Educating the Emotionally Disturbed Child" and "Guiding the Emotionally Disturbed Child" became some of the most well-attended classes during the late 60s and into the 70s. He also taught a "Psychology of Delinquency" class. Nick held the adjunct professor position at Xavier University until 2011. He never missed a semester or one class in all the years he taught at Xavier.

Changes in mental health in the early 70's led Nick to accept a position as the court administrator to Judge John O'Connor at the Hamilton County Juvenile Court in Cincinnati and later under Judge Tom Lipps. His speaking engagements and card shows continued, always with education and children in mind. Nick retired from this position in 1998. In his later years, he did marriage counseling with the goal of keeping the marriage together. In addition to his classes at Xavier, Nick also taught at Northern Kentucky University from 1977 to 2007. He also taught leadership courses for the Army in Kansas City, Missouri. He was capable of taking the most mundane material and making it zing. He truly believed Solomon's words, "There's nothing new under the sun," and used the simplest of concepts to help his classes, audiences and everyone he met feel they could bless others just by being *real* and *caring*.

Nick continued throughout his life to use his passion for teaching and speaking for the benefit of many children in need at the Children's Unit School, Millcreek and the Hamilton County Juvenile Court. At home, Nick enjoyed a robust family life. He raised four sons and five daughters who he believed were the most brilliant, intelligent and wonderful children in the world.

He was an encourager to everyone he met. The presentation of his personality was dynamic. When Nick Seta entered the room, his presence was felt, especially by those who received a hearty slap on the back or poke in the chest along with his energetic greetings. As his cousin John reflected, "You wanted more of his presence."

Nick's presence is dearly missed, though we take comfort in his faith. And until we see him again, he has left us the legacy of his words and encouragement. – Lynn Seta

# The Talks

"I'm not here to bring you anything new, I purposely limit myself to common sense" N.S.

# The Talks

Nick was a very popular speaker throughout Ohio, Kentucky, Indiana and other states. There were several years that he was asked to speak over two hundred times. He spoke to various groups: women's groups, men's groups, all kinds of teacher groups, librarians, nurses, church groups, political groups, and student groups. For a while, he flew to Kansas City yearly to teach officers in the military. His topics stayed consistent. One of his first and most popular was "The Ten Commandments of Surface Behavior" along with "Productive Personality" and "Discipline." He spoke about listening, motivation, communication and leadership. He spoke to church groups about guilt, marriage, and parenting, along with his other talks tailored from a biblical perspective.

He often combined several of his talks to meet the requests of his audience. There were also talks early on in Nick's career about materialism, the dangers of pornography, and of course, his work at the Children's Unit School at Longview State Hospital. These particular talks helped enormously with the funding programs at the school, the purchase of vans, and field trips for the socially, emotionally, and educationally impoverished group of children he served. Along with his educational talks, he entertained audiences with his "An Exposé of Gambling." As well as entertaining, there was a serious educational component of how we all can be cheated with a deck of cards.

Nick often gave this disclaimer in his teaching and talks. He said, "I'm not here to bring you anything new. I purposely limit myself to common sense. That's what wisdom is: an uncommon amount of common sense. I know you know the material in the handout. But in the area of behavior, the issue is not what you know but the issue is what you do. What do you do with what you know? I do not challenge your knowledge of this material but rather your awareness of how well you do it."

# Common Sense about Kids

"Role modeling is not an occasional example. It is a patterned example ever present for others to imitate."
N.S.

# TALK #1
# The Ten Commandments of Surface Behavior

As individuals influencing the lives of youngsters, we must have a strong, personal philosophy about what we are doing. It must be a philosophy of which we are completely convinced. Our field is rampant with theories of how we should teach, discipline and motivate a kid. If we are not strong in our own thoughts and feelings, we will end up floundering and frustrated.

Why should we teach children to decode and deal with their own behavior? Because...

- Behavior is the key to getting the most out of life.
- Behavior defines us. Behavior determines our quality of life.
- The only thing that alters behavior is consequences.
- The choices we make, make us.
- Our efforts are like seeds; they germinate, grow roots, and then, sometimes, produce the plant.

Finally, we should teach children to have insight into the connection between thoughts and behavior. It all starts with thought. Our mind is the rehearsal hall for our actions. Our words set the stage.

*Our thoughts lead to Words,*
*which lead to Feelings,*
*which lead to Actions,*
*which lead to Habits,*
*that develop our Character,*
*which determines our Destiny.*

## Commandment 1:
## Know your purpose, right, responsibility and philosophy

I recommend a philosophy of influence that explains our purpose, our right and our responsibility. Our purpose is to direct and redirect the behavior of youngsters in a manner effective and comfortable to us as managers, and healthy and productive for the children in our care. The definition of our right is the sensitive and personal right of guiding and controlling the behavior of other human beings. Another term for this would be the right of management. Finally, our responsibilities are to foster reciprocal dignity and to engage in role modeling. In exercising our right of management, we must accept the responsibilities that are attached to that right. Having adopted this philosophy, we can allow it to play out in the following practical strategies for influencing behavior.

## Commandment 2:
## Sometimes it's better not to see or hear

Planned ignoring is the ability to select which behavior to intervene with and which to ignore. You cannot interfere with all of your children's behaviors and be effective. This technique permits the dissipation of tensions allowing youngsters to stop their own behavior.

## Commandment 3:
## Use a sign, sound, or look

In many instances, a word or motion provides enough intervening support to enable youngsters to handle their impulses. Actions such as yelling, cursing, moving, et cetera, can be stopped by a simple sign, sound or look. So often, we raise the roof when we need only to raise our eyebrows. Through these subtle means, a good influencer asserts control of the environment. By contrast, screamers and yellers never learn that no one listens or even hears.

## Commandment 4:
## Get 'em over the hump

It is the well-timed boost given to kids helping them over a hump blocking their way to a goal. This often spells the difference between a rage outburst and success. If help is given at the right moment, youngsters are usually able to go on, and their undesirable behavior is prevented.

## Commandment 5:
## Be just

If you do not witness an incident, handle all parties alike, ignore or give equal treatment. Kids consistently desire fairness from adults. A message from kids would be something like, "Be fair. If we perceive you as fair, we will buy what you're doing. It doesn't mean we like it. But if we perceive you as unfair, watch out! Problems are coming."

Being fair means you react to behavior with facts and knowledge, not bias and prejudice. For instance, you have a good boy and a bad boy involved, and you just know it is the bad boy's fault. Do You? The kids know you don't know. Let me give you an example. I have three sons. I hear problems in the next room and walk in to see what's going on. The oldest points to the other two. "I didn't do anything." Number two and three say the same thing. Being a good Italian father, they are all in big trouble. You might think that's not fair to the little one. Actually, another lesson can be taught in this circumstance. We must teach, and they must learn, you are guilty by association. Strive for intelligent judgments, not emotional reactions.

## Commandment 6:
## Become one of their fans

Build your kids up by showing interest in their work, projects, play, etc. Exude praise and amazement over their accomplishments. They love phrases such as, "Did you do that by yourself?" "When did you get that good?" "Is this really yours?" The human ego is a bottomless pit in the area of praise and recognition. It is the only human need that can never be satisfied.

Remember, praise improves hearing. I can hear praise 100 feet away but not what my wife said, standing right next to me.

## Commandment 7:
## Follow the rules for good rules

A good rule is specific. Tell children what you want. Keep procedures simple and avoid vague rules. (Examples of vague rules include "Don't go too far," "Don't be too late," "Don't stay on the phone too long," and the best, "Be Good.") A good rule is simple. Complexity lends itself to confusion and leaves youngsters with only one option–to act out either externally or internally. Good rules are consistently enforced. An organized routine tells kids what is expected of them and what they can expect in return. Remember, all kids don't process language at the same rate and manner. You should not expect the kid to understand rules through inference, deduction or intuition. The instructional process should be neither challenging nor confusing.

## Commandment 8:
## Save your threats

Making threats causes the relationship between you and the child to become adversarial. We usually regret making them. We make them when we are angry. We say we're going to do things we cannot do, should not do or do not even want to do. Threats move us from a position of power to one of no choice. We put the trigger in the hands of the youngsters. We need to deal in consequences, not threats.

## Commandment 9:
## Use the positive rather than the negative

Too often, we violate this rule by ignoring youngsters until they misbehave, thus focusing our attention on incorrect behavior. We use negative statements of control such as "Take your feet off the chair" when we should say the positive instruction of "Put your feet on the floor." Negative statements do not tell a youngster what to do and have the added problem of setting up opportunities for malicious obedience.

Here's an example of how we can use the positive rather than the negative in an intentional way. Let's say you and your friend are inside talking and you check on the children. The four are playing nicely. You silently sneak away from the window. Why don't you now grab a tray of cookies and go to the children? Say, "You are playing so well, have a cookie!" When you leave, they say to each other "Wow, let's play good some more!"

# Commandment 10:
# Become an artist

Managing and coordinating human behavior is pure art. Artists cause change and leave an imprint.

# TALK #2
# Become A Master Artist: The Fine Art of Molding Human Behavior

Whether one is parenting, teaching or engaging in some other work with children, managing and coordinating human behavior is pure art. Molding, guiding and controlling human behavior is the most demanding of all the arts. Artists cause *change* and leave an *imprint*. Masters in the art of molding behavior promote development and progress in the child. The goal is continuous growth and that goal requires ongoing self-assessment.

Rome was not built in a day, nor is a human person. We start out as kids. So always think of kids as developing adults. Our most important possession is our behavior. It renders everything else moot. For example, what good is talent, status or wealth to a person who can't behave himself? In raising children, we must push the behavioral bar as much as the academic bar. EQ is as important as IQ. Intelligence guides us. Emotions rule us. That's why we do wrong even when we know it's not right.

> You want to see change in the kids you are leading, then live by one axiom:
> *"Be the change you want to see."*

**Are you a "Change Agent?"**
- A Change Agent has a Philosophy: I will do my very best to give others the opportunity to make the right choices.
- A Change Agent is a Role Model: I will do more than, better than, and more consistently than anything I demand of others.
- A Change Agent is a Self-Actualized Person: I will actually do my actual best with what I actually have; that I will do and teach children to do the right thing, at the right time, in the right way, for the right reason.

Teachers (or parents) teach through their speech, model through their behavior, and demand through their personal discipline. Increase in the numbers of "difficult" kids and their unacceptable behavior tells us that kids are suffering from a lack of healthy role models because everything we do is learned behavior. We learn by watching others. That's why role models are so important. Role modeling is not an occasional example. It is a patterned example ever present for others to imitate. Kids choose their own role models. You might just be the only 'healthy' role model in their life.

## The Artist's Toolkit

- Kids respect sharpness and power.
- Use the power of affectionate and enthusiastic utterance.
- Drill reinforcement is essential to learning.
- Don't tell kids how wrong they are; teach them how right they can be.
- Help kids improve their self-perception. We are what we believe we are.

The art of molding human behavior is the art of assigning consequences for actions. In fact, the only thing that alters human behavior, positively or negatively, is a consequence. In order for consequences to be right and effective in shaping behavior, a kid must know what actions will bring, understand the idea of cause and effect and be capable of making behavior choices. For example, the behavior of getting and keeping a job will lead to the consequence of:

- Having cash to spend,
- Having somewhere to be other than on the streets,
- Financing a college degree.

On the other hand, what consequences come from choosing a path other than working for a living? Convince kids to get a job and keep a job.

Superior teachers believe in the power of affectionate and enthusiastic utterance, which helps kids to recognize and manage their own behavior and then make good decisions. The first step is to manage your presuppositions and expectations. The first presupposition is about the health of children with problem behavior. These kids are difficult, but they are not sick. They are capable of learning right from wrong and are capable of making right and wrong choices. It's important we believe this because as teachers, we must be free to demand, not ask or request. We must track academics, appropriate behavior, and daily responsibilities. We will not feel free to do so if we believe they are sick.

The next presupposition is one held by the children themselves. We must manage what a child thinks, feels or believes about himself. Behavior is absolutely impacted by self-perception. If a child thinks he is ugly, dumb, and mistreated, that will influence his behavior. Here is a caveat: chance or circumstance influence, which is to say, increases your want to do it, but they do not determine your behavior. In other words, *nothing* made you do a behavior but you.

The most efficient way to reduce maladaptive behavior is to help kids improve their self-perception by teaching them how to become responsible, productive and significant. These are the essential ingredients of human dignity. Do not limit your responsibilities to academic success. You must teach the whole child. The behavioral bar must be as high or higher than the academic bar.

## Fundamental Principles of the Artist

There are many guiding principles for adults working with kids, but here are three special ones for all who practice the art of shaping kids' behavior. First, we must constantly increase our knowledge and understanding of behavior. Why? This is what enables us to develop strategies and opportunities for kids to change their own behavior. They must learn to change their own behavior.

The second fundamental principle is to attend to the method for identifying behavior that needs help. We need to observe, record, and refer in a professional manner. Be aware of your own biases and prejudices.

The third fundamental principle is to be disciplined in our informal interactions with kids as well as formal ones. For example, whenever or wherever we relate to kids, be it at recess, in the dining room, et cetera, we must not minimize or oversimplify the problems of kids. We must also limit ourselves to our capabilities and training. Resist the urge to reduce all problems to a moral or educational issue. It is also important to maintain confidentiality except for the greater good.

Become an artist whose media are speech, behavior and personal discipline. Teach with your enthusiastic utterances. Be a healthy role model with your behavior and your own personal discipline. Teach what you know by doing what you know. Who you are determines the effectiveness of what you are. To create the masterpiece of desired behavior from a difficult kid, make sure your manner is right, your motive is right, and your message is right.

# TALK #3
# Causes or Changes:
# Two Approaches to Analysis

There are two main schools of thought to the approach of how to study and improve human behavior. They are *behavioral analysis*, based on the research and conclusions of B.F. Skinner and *psychoanalysis*, based on the work of Sigmund Freud. They are similar in that both are analytical and both agree that past experiences cause current behaviors. The psychoanalysts maintain that past experiences cause current behavior by channeling unconscious mental forces into action. What is my reaction to analysis being a viable approach to improving behavior?

I guess if you pin me down, I'm not an advocate of the analytical approach to behavior. Over the long haul, I don't buy what it's saying. I don't believe the underlying premise that we are subject to and controlled by intra-psychic forces of which we're not even aware; that we are victims of our *environment* and our *unconscious*. I have a rough time with this because when you begin to wallow in this kind of mystical rationale you end up with the garbage of ignoring the reality of *individual choices* and *personal responsibility*.

## Causes or Changes

After many years of participating and observing others

in attempting to equate cause of behavior with early life experiences, I've come to believe that knowing the *causes* have very little to do with *changing the behavior*. Quite often I've felt it works in reverse; we use it as a cop-out. Look at how many criminals have learned to use their past to justify their criminal activities. Asking "Why?" has become equivalent to leading with your chin.

Seeking causes in the scientific world is proper. Once you know why something happens you have a principle that allows you to control or predict the phenomenon. If you attempt to apply this to the infinite reactions of the human personality, you end up with either simplistic or misleading conclusions.

It is well and good to have a realization of the *why* of behavior, but we must then get to the *what* are we going to do about it and get the damned thing done.

My attitude and philosophy is to teach kids that significant behaviors are not the result of chance or circumstance. They are the result of choice. Chance and circumstance can and do *influence us*, but they do not *determine us*.

## Building Character to Shape Behavior

Our mission as parents, teachers and caregivers is to help youngsters become 1. Morally and socially competent, 2. Marketable, and 3. Self-Reliant. To accomplish this with some degree of success, one must be attractive to their world. There are four main areas of attractiveness: physical, talent, character, and behavior. Unfortunately, our culture emphasizes and romanticizes the first two: diets, fitness centers, cosmetics, hair, plastic surgery, et cetera, put a very emphatic focus on physical attraction. Adulation of the athlete, entertainer, movie and T.V. star, celebrities, et cetera, promotes the glamorization of talent. The message kids receive is, "If you are sexy and or talented, you can say what you want, do what you want, and be what you want." To the kid, there is no greater, seductive message. That is their dream, to be able to say, do and be whatever you feel like.

The last two areas of attractiveness, character and

behavior, are the essence and substance of our human nature. They are much more important than the first two, but are, unfortunately, ignored and minimized.

### Four Guiding Principles of Character and Behavior

1. Talent is a blessing, but talent without character is a curse.
2. Talent gets you to the top; character keeps you there.
3. The worst thing that can happen to you is to make it on the outside before you make it on the inside.
4. There is no good deal on the outside if you haven't got a good deal on the inside.

# TALK #4
# Discipline for Teens

Discipline is a group of ideas, thoughts, and actions structured to produce success. This demands the consistent enforcement of the standards necessary to that structure. The goal of disciplining children is to teach them appropriate social and moral behavior. Regardless of the circumstance or situation, they are to do the right thing, in the right way, at the right time, for the right reason. We are going to discuss guiding principles that help us in this pursuit.

*Definition of Self-Control: Do the right thing, in the right way, at the right time, for the right reason.*

## What is Discipline?

Simply stated, discipline is the teaching and enforcing of standards. The goal of discipline is self-discipline, which is achieved through guidance and practice. You must demand that kids behave in a manner that is in harmony with the collective good of society. They must understand that if they want privileges and protection, they must accept limits. As long as they are in the stage of taking, they are not going to dictate the rules. Make certain they understand your rules, be prepared to discuss them and be willing to change a rule if you see that it needs changing. Do not be intimidated by teenage sophistication and self-assurance.

Be the wall kids do not break down. Do not allow them to make decisions they are not ready to make. Delegate responsibility to them as soon as they are capable. This transmits trust. As they grow, so do their demands. Don't strain your ears waiting to hear logic, reason or sanity from the mouths of your teenagers when you set limits for curfew, dress, choice of friends, hangouts, et cetera. The essence of discipline is rooted in manifested concern. Kids must know it is because you care for them that you will not allow them to run into danger. They must know that you care enough to care. You must believe that children who are dependent upon you must obey. You must be fair by making certain that kids know, understand and are capable of doing what you expect of them. Responsibility must be reciprocal.

Adolescence is an unstable time. The struggle for values can be bewildering and devastating. Kids are bombarded with the propaganda that everybody in their age group likes and dislikes the same things, does drugs, alcohol, and sex, and if they don't, they're not with it and out of the loop. It is called peer pressure. You've got to help kids handle this pressure by providing strategies, choices, and the guts to take a stand. But you must also take a stand when you are on stage and hear that "Everybody's doing it." Stand for what you know is right. You must always be able to say, "I did my best to give them the opportunity to make the right choice." This at least assures you of not having regrets, the one satisfaction you must have when struggling with your kids.

## Pursuing Discipline, Three Guiding Principles

### 1. Tell Kids What You Want
Kids are not mind-readers. Do not expect kids to know what you want through some inductive, deductive or inferential process. Express yourself in a clear, firm, and reasonable manner. Be specific. Vague rules are seductive. Where do you stand in areas of language, punctuality, dress, tasks, curfew, movies, et cetera?

"Rules" such as straighten up your room, no rough-housing, don't go too far or stay too long, or out too late are not rules at all because they are vague. The best example of this is the rule "be good." Compared to whom, Al Capone?

## 2. Be Sure Your Rules Are Known and Understood

Kids must know what to do before they can do it. To make certain your rules are known and understood, do the following with the rules: a) review b) restate c) post. Discuss your rules with an experienced and honest friend. Respect experience. Seek advice and opinion.

## 3. Give Consequences

The only thing that alters behavior is consequences. Without consequences, actions have no meaning.

*Effective Consequences*

Rules without consequences soon become empty threats. Nothing undermines behavior management more than empty threats. Kids do not respect adults who allow them to violate rules. They do respect adults who allow them to make a mistake and help them correct it, however, an adult who allows a kid to repeatedly make the same "mistake" is failing at consequences.

It is our responsibility to instill healthy fear. It stops you from doing what is wrong and starts you doing what is right. To be effective, consequences must be immediate and meaningful. Don't let it pile up until you hear yourself saying something like, "I've had it up to here."

*Giving Correction*

Positive correction is best. Positive correction is accomplished through constructive teaching. Instead of "stop being late," which focuses on the negative, teach them the positive behavior of how to be on time. Teach them to set an alarm, fix lunch the night before, lay out clothes the night before, et cetera. Kids will correct themselves with a positive attitude because they know you care. Telling kids what not to do sets you up for malicious obedience. Instead avoid negative statements. For example, say, "Let's keep our feet on the floor" instead of "Don't put your feet on the chair." Or say "Let's hang our coats on the hooks" instead of "Don't leave your coat on the chair."

Correct the behavior, not the person. Do not demean the person. This is easy to do when you don't like the kid. Flee from statements such as, "How can you be so stupid?" or "What is wrong with you?" or "Can't you do anything right?" Simply correct the wrong and teach the right. Be aware of self-fulfilling prophecies. Once we make such judgments about a kid, we need to prove ourselves right.

*Yes and No*

Establish this understanding of your 'yes' and 'no' very early! Teach them that when you say 'yes' it's because you love them, and it's the right thing to do, and when you say 'no' it's because you love them and it's not the right thing to do. Do not allow 'no' to become a discussion. If you do, you will be enabling regressive behavior. You will teach your children to get what they want by creating emotional pressure—through nagging, whining and complaining.

Here are two basic rules to follow. First, whenever possible, say 'yes.' For example, say 'yes' to kids going out to play 20 minutes before supper. The second rule is try to provide an acceptable alternative to what you have not permitted. For example, if a girl wants to go to a movie Friday night but at a location that is inappropriate for her age, offer a movie at home instead. You could allow boys to join her; you could peek in on them and offer refreshments.

One final word for successful discipline is consistency. Consistency is the heart and soul of discipline. Something can't be okay today and not the next. Consistency breeds security. It lets kids know you are fair and where you stand. Inconsistency breeds insecurity and anarchy.

# TALK #5
# Solving the Puzzle of Failing Children

Allow me to preface these thoughts by explaining that I will refer to all of you as teachers because if an adult relates to a child in a consistent adult/child relationship, they become teachers to that child. I will refer to you as leaders because when you are in charge of another person, you become a leader. I will refer to you as role models because that's the greatest responsibility you have to others. I will refer to Christ's teachings.

Teaching the *whole child* means modeling and teaching life skills. By life skills, I mean teaching about making good decisions, respecting others and working is a must. Many kids in urban areas have school problems in their early years that lead to social problems in later years. Verbalized solutions to these problems are better facilities, teachers, curriculums, government policies, et cetera. These areas are necessary but not sufficient. Factors that enable kids to have a decent shot at succeeding in school are much more basic. For instance, a decent home gets them to bed on time, gets them up on time, sees that they have clean clothes and breakfast. A decent home requires study completion of homework, helps kids get to school punctually and encourages obedience to their teachers. These are the things that lead to school success and, later, to social success. It's not money, buildings, politicians, et cetera; it's good old parental involvement.

Kids need stable homes. Kids that come from traditional families have far less involvement in school failure, illegitimate parenting, crime, unemployment, and defiance of authority. Schools can only rise to the level of parental quality. Together, parents and schools can teach kids the importance of reliability, accountability and willingness, the core ingredients of character. Together they can reach into the medicine cabinet and give kids a strong dose of personal appearance, politeness, punctuality, promptness, perseverance, and pride. These are the core ingredients of social success.

Parents in urban school districts must step up their attendance at parent-teacher conferences and involvement in school functions. If they do not, their complaints lack credibility, and nothing changes.

Kids must realize they have to contribute. When schools and parents are doing their best, kids must do their best. When urban schools were doing a good job, this was the way it was. If kids didn't do their work and got bad grades, they were held responsible and paid the consequences. We've moved away from that position. Now all we hear is that it's the fault of schools, teachers, insufficient books, school boards, et cetera. It is no longer the kids. This is a fatal mistake. Kids are over-joyed when someone else is blamed for their behavior.

In her article titled, "We all have to get involved to improve schools," *Cincinnati Enquirer* writer Krista Ramsey stated, "There is, curiously enough, no indicator that measures how hard students are willing to work or how involved parents are in their children's education. Yet many foreign educational systems, especially those regularly mentioned as kicking U.S. schools' behinds, cite such things as the basis of their success."

The puzzle is made up of schools, parents, and kids. The most important piece is parental involvement.

# TALK #6
# Differences in Difficult Kids

What do we mean by "Difficult Youngsters?" This term describes kids who have great difficulty meeting their desires, wishes, and demands in a manner that is acceptable and satisfying to both them and society. They are impulse driven.

Such children present a major problem to our society because their means of getting what they want can lead to violent crime. Violent crime affects our quality of life; we limit where we let our kids go, lock our cars and are cautious where we drive. Our homes have special locks, alarms, dogs and weapons. Teens up to age nineteen make up a large percentage of our violent crime.

The mental health problems of "difficult" kids are a staggering societal problem as well. Outcomes include institutionalization, drug and alcohol abuse and suicides. Boys suffer from these problems at 5 times the rate of girls.

## Things They Don't Do Well

*Delayed Gratification*

There are certain behaviors necessary to personal development that difficult kids have problems with. The following is a brief discussion of three important ones. To begin, the difficult child has trouble delaying immediate gratification. Humans are genetically coded for immediate gratification. It springs from our selfish nature. We are self-orbiting creatures. We want what we want immediately, if not sooner. We all must be taught to control and channel our desires and demands in a socially acceptable manner. We all need to hear, "Not the right time." "Not in this situation." "We all have to wait." Don't just say "no." When possible, explain.

Kids raised in a healthy environment learn to accept "no." Difficult kids do not; they are much more volatile. Due to their paranoid-like thinking, they will accuse you of unfairness, discrimination, and rejection. They will accuse you of not liking them or that you like others more than you like them. They systematize these beliefs in a manner that enables them to justify their behavior. They will often ask for things they know you must say "No" to in order to prove their point.

*Seeking Help*

The next disadvantage for difficult kids is they are not good at seeking help. Most humans do not like to seek help. We start demanding our independence early in life. Before we can do anything, we're saying we can do everything; "I can go to the bathroom, I can tie my shoes, I can zip my zipper, I can feed myself." Long before we can do any of these things, we want to be grown-up and solve our own problems. We despise seeking help because of our pride; we attach failure and weakness to needing help. This all gets compounded because we, very early in life, come to the conclusion that all adults are stupid, old fashioned, and just don't understand. However, kids raised in a healthy environment soon learn to seek help. They come to realize they can't do all the things they think they can, and more importantly, they have adults around ready to help them. They have the opportunity to practice and develop the ability to seek help.

By contrast, difficult kids, who often do not come from healthy environments, do not have willing, helpful adults around. They develop the belief that no one really wants to help them, so why should they ask? The end result is that they do not have the opportunity or motivation to be proactive and develop the ability to seek help. Difficult kids avoid seeking help.

*Guilt*

Finally, difficult kids handle guilt poorly. Normal guilt is necessary for the formation and maintenance of productive, healthy relationships. When we do unwarranted things that are hurtful and damaging to others, we should have feelings of sorrow and regret. It is called conscience. Freud called it Super Ego. Kids raised in healthy environments have a better opportunity to develop a healthy conscience.

Internalized guilt causes irritation that seeks relief. However, kids, especially difficult kids, externalize rather than internalize. Instead of admission, they substitute projection to blame others. For example, the child externalizing his guilt may say something like, "I didn't start fighting till he hit me back." Instead of correction, they substitute rationalization to justify their actions. Instead of regret and sorrow, they use reversal to make others guilty for their behavior. "If you had bought me the CD player, I wouldn't have had to steal it."

Family, neighborhood, church, and school all contribute to the necessary teaching that it's right and okay to feel guilty. We can't make them feel, but we can tell them how they should feel. Then the child with the guilty feelings will be motivated to seek relief. Now we can tell the child that he should seek forgiveness to be freed from his guilt and feel better.

Pride makes it very difficult for us to ask for forgiveness because it makes us vulnerable. Why? Because asking for forgiveness demands admission or confession. Then a change of mind, change of heart, and change of behavior must take place (this is also called repentance). Finally, we must be contrite. Contrition is to feel regret or sorrow for our actions.

Beware of false confessions such as "I said I did it, so you shouldn't punish me!" And also note that some kids may give a false apology that blames others. This is not true contrition.

## A few remarks to kids

If you think teachers are tough, wait until you get a boss. When you mess up they don't ask, "How do you feel about it?" "Are you Okay?" Bosses are not interested in helping you find yourself.
- Life isn't fair. . . . So? Get used to it.
- The real world does not give you your self-esteem. The real world demands that you earn your self-esteem.
- You're not entitled to make $40,000 right out of high school.
- If you screw up, it's not your parent's fault. It's you.
- Your parents weren't always boring and slow. They got that way paying your bills, doing your laundry, cleaning your room and listening to your complaints.
- Schools may not believe in winners and losers, but life does. Schools may give you many chances to get it right. Life doesn't.
- Be nice to your nerd friends. You might end up working for one of them.
- Before you start saving the world, delouse your bedroom closet.
- Teen years are great. Enjoy them before you too, become one of hose boring, slow, obnoxious parents.

## A few remarks from kids to parents
- Be consistent. When you are inconsistent, I lose faith and trust in you.
- Be firm. It makes me feel safe.
- Let me take reasonable risks and experience consequences. At times learning hurts, but that's the way I grow.
- Don't pick my friends apart. They are important to me.
- If you are wrong, apologize. When you do, I respect you more than you'll ever know.
- When you tell me you're going to do something, please do it.

- If possible, don't correct me in front of others.
- Stop me when I'm doing the wrong thing. Habits are hard to break.
- Answer my questions whenever you can; I have faith and trust in you.
- When you correct me, please teach me.

# Common Sense about Leadership

"Our mind is the rehersal hall for our actions" N.S.

# TALK #7
# Leadership Point of View

You can be given the position of leadership, but not the qualities of leadership—those you must earn. The driving force in a leader is his internal desire to use his power and authority for the benefit of others. Leadership is internal. It comes from the inside out, not the outside in. Leadership is attitude, an attitude that radiates the desire to lead. It is the willingness to step out and take intelligent risks and not be afraid to make mistakes. Leadership is persona, a persona that projects high achievement, optimism, perseverance, and passion—especially the passion for helping others overcome and succeed. The emphasis of our discussion will not be the pragmatics of leadership, such as systems, strategies, time, execution, assessments, et cetera. These all are important but are not the essence of leadership. Our emphasis will be on the spirit driving the pragmatics.

**Role Modeling**

Leaders are role models. Everything we do is learned behavior. We learn by watching others. Role modeling is not an occasional example. It is a patterned example ever-present for others to imitate. What is role modeling? Role modeling is the impact that your behavior has on others.

What exactly are you saying when you accept the responsibility of a role model (which is to say when you accept a position of leadership)? You are saying, "I will do more than, better than, and more consistently than anything I demand of others."

Why is role modeling so important? It earns you the right to demand. Leadership, by its very nature, demands that you demand because people, by their very nature, will cause you to demand. Your position gives you authority, but you must not rely solely on the authority of position to be forceful. That is dictatorship, not leadership. The only way you earn the right to influence the behavior of others is through your own behavior.

What is the "goal" of role modeling? The goal is to teach and emphasize the importance of doing the right thing in the right way, at the right time, and most importantly, for the right reason.

Remember these closing observations about role-modeling in leadership.

- People always watch and observe those in charge. A smile signals acceptance and approval.
- The sermon seen is much more powerful than the sermon heard.
- An example is not the best way to teach behaviors; it is the only way.
- Teach what you know by doing what you know.

## Role Modeling for Children

Children learn how to behave by watching others. Your behavior will have an impact on children as they watch you. What impact will your behavior have on them? For kids, their peer group is also a role model. You must emphasize, "Right is right even when no one else is doing it, and wrong is wrong even when everyone else is doing it." Our responsibility is not to prepare a future for our kids. Our responsibility is to prepare kids for the future.

## Self-Assessment

The evaluation of one's self is the lifeline of leadership. This is what enables us to improve ourselves. It is the only way we change ourselves. It is the best way to know when we need a kick in the pants. It's far better for us to know and do these things for ourselves before others oblige us.

Leaders do not believe in being accidentally good or accidentally bad. They live by the motto, "I'm good today, but I'll be better tomorrow." They don't want to start slipping. They realize the proverbial slippery slope gets slipperier going down. Daily self-assessment prevents this by causing you to correct and improve a little bit at a time on the little things. It's the little things that count. Take care of the good little things, and the big bad things won't happen.

As a leader, you must subject yourself to the uncomfortable question at the end of each day; "Did I actually do my actual best with what I actually had?" If you can consistently answer "yes," you will not be a victim of stress and will not be a failure. If your answer is "no," you are going to drift, lose focus, and take things for granted. Be a victim of stress, and you will be a failure.

**Choice and Philosophy**

I've lumped these two together because of the importance of choice. We make choices every day: some good, some bad. Choice determines our quality of life. The choices we make, make us. Remember this sequence:

**THOUGHTS**
⬇
**FEELINGS**
⬇
**ACTIONS**
⬇
**HABITS**
⬇
**CHARACTER**
⬇
**DESTINY**

It all starts with a thought. Our mind is the rehearsal hall for our actions.

With this background, I sought to answer the fundamental question: What philosophical principle should form the basis of my efforts toward others? I arrived at the following conclusion. "I will do my best to give others the opportunity to make the right choice."

We cannot cause others to do anything. Causation is the result of an internal desire. Do not confuse this with compliance, which is the result of external forces. Causation results from internalization. Compliance results from concession. I am belaboring this point to emphasize that our responsibility is to provide the opportunity while causation is the individual's responsibility. In the area of behavior, do not demand internal results for your efforts. You can want and hope for them but not demand it of them. If you demand, you will burn out. You cannot change others. Only they can do that. Remember how difficult it is to change yourself when straining to change others.

**Set the Stage**

While leaders cannot force people to change, they can set the stage for success. You can develop a culture that motivates people to want to work together to achieve the best results for the good of all. To do this, leaders must:

- Choose the right people for the right roles and turn them loose.
- Set the example, develop relationships, and exercise communication.
- Use common sense.

Common sense is when intuition and intelligence come together. You have training and experience, the two ingredients that spawn intuition. Trust your intuition because leaders must take risks, and risks are based on intuitiveness.

Intelligence, emotions, and physical desires influence

decisions. They must be kept in balance, but in the final analysis, intelligence must govern. If emotions and body are allowed to rule, history has taught us that they do not produce the best results.

## Security and Significance

More than ever before, we all seek security and significance. Whom do we trust anymore: Politics, education, judicial, church, media, law enforcement, corporate world? These pillars of our outer world gave support and comfort to our inner world. That's no longer true. As a result, individual personal relationships have become increasingly important to us, and one of the most important of our daily relationships is the one we have with our direct supervisor in the workplace. We all want leaders who care and are reliable because caring and reliability are the parents of security and significance.

# TALK #8
# Listen to Them

God created us as relational beings with a sense of community and the need to reach out to others. The pervasive obstacle that blocks our way to achieving this is our innate narcissism, which is to say, our excessive fascination with ourselves. Narcissism and being relational cannot coexist. Christ knew this and helped us by spending much time in his teaching ministry on behavior. He spent time on the importance of example, actions, giving, forgiving, serving, power, et cetera. Behavior, behavior, behavior!

In His sermons, parables, and teachings, Christ wove the following behavior messages:

- For relational beings, their most important possession is their behavior. It describes us, but more importantly, it defines us.
- Relational people must be behaviorally attractive. We are not drawn to critical, complaining, cynical people. We are drawn to people who are courteous, complimentary, patient, and kind.
- We're drawn to those who do the right things for the right reason. Relational people must always seek and adopt attractive behaviors. That is what we are doing in this narrative. We are discussing a behavioral quality that

is vital, attractive, and necessary to the development of being relational.

## Listening

Scripture emphasizes listening. *Proverbs 1:5* says, "Let the wise listen and add to their learning, and let the discerning get guidance." Why does listening occupy such a high place on the ladder of relationships? That's a good question that has a good answer. Listening in and of itself incorporates several attractive behaviors and contains a formula for succeeding:

$$P + P \text{ and } C + C = \text{Success.}$$

The first P is for *politeness*. Human society has always attached significance to politeness. We judge children and young people by it. We admire and praise polite adults. Will Rogers said it best when he wrote, "Politeness is to the human being what heat is to wax. It melts us." We are attracted by the respect and humility attached to politeness. Politeness and effective listening are inseparable.

The second P in the formula is for *patience*. We love patient people. They make us feel worthwhile and valuable. They make us feel they like us and want us to succeed. We like people who like us. One of the best-known and most quoted verses in the bible begins with "Love is patient." We are attracted to the passion inherent in patience. Patience and effective listening are inseparable.

The two Cs are for *care* and *concern*. We value people who care enough to be aware of our needs and are concerned enough to want to do something about them. We are highly attracted by the energy and effort that goes into care and concern. Care, concern, and effective listening are inseparable.

Obviously, effective listening plays a major role in our development as relational beings. It would be well to define it. Meaning is best served by definition. Effective listening simply means that when someone is speaking to us, we are to do our best to convince that person that we are trying to understand what they are telling us; that we really want to grasp their entire message.

We are not just hearing their words; we are also listening to the ideas, thoughts, and feelings attached to those words. This is no easy task. To accomplish it, you must listen with your eyes as well as your ears because when we speak, only about 10% of our meaning is in our words, about 40% is in the tone of our voice, and the remaining 50% is in various nonverbal actions such as hand motions, head nods, facial expressions, et cetera. Remember humans are masters of the mask. We are quite good at masking our feelings and thoughts behind our words. That's why we are so adept at saying one thing while actually feeling and thinking another.

There are four verbal communication skills: reading, writing, speaking, and listening. Half of our communication time is taken up by spelling, reading and writing. The other part of communication is listening alone.

Two brilliant interpreters of human behavior, Milton and Shakespeare, set the table for us. Milton said, "The noblest of our daily activities is to listen to understand." Shakespeare said, "The most romantic thing we can do for one another is to listen." These two men attached the virtue of romance and nobility to listening because they understood the importance of self-respect, for which we will do anything; without self-respect, we are nothing. The inherent importance of self-respect is contained in the proposition that we need to believe our ideas are interesting, our thoughts are intelligent, and our feelings are important. Nothing validates that proposition better or quicker than effective listening. Effective listening gratifies our need for self-respect. Anyone who does this for us on a consistent level will be effective and will influence us.

### Influence and Leadership

I write the word influence, and my mind immediately transitions to leadership. Christ demands leadership (see *Matthew 28:19*).

## The Four Cornerstones of Leadership

### Influence

The first cornerstone is *influence*. Leaders influence by role modeling. Christ demands role modeling (see *Matthew 5:16*). He is teaching us that leaders must earn the right to influence the behavior of others through their own behavior. People always watch the people in charge.

### Relationships

The second cornerstone is *relationships*. Relationships take time. Leaders find and take the time to relate. An outstanding example of this was General "Ike" Eisenhower. While in England, preparing to launch the greatest military operation in history, he would, several times a week, go down to the parade grounds where hundreds of soldiers were training for the invasion. As his jeep came onto the scene, everyone came to a halt and stood at attention. Ike would stride through the ranks of troops, establish eye contact, and flash his famous grin to as many soldiers as he could. Then he would go front and center to a raised podium and address the entire body. When he got back to headquarters, he would always remark that relating to the soldiers was the finest use of his time. Leaders find and take the time to relate.

### Communication

The third cornerstone is *communication*. Leaders communicate. They understand that in communication there are two elements: sending and receiving. Leaders know when to stand, speak, and send. They also know when to sit, listen, and receive. They value and appreciate the thoughts of others. Leaders communicate.

## Resolution

The fourth cornerstone is *resolution*. When all the networking and team building is done, leaders know a decision must be made. Leaders embrace making decisions. They anticipate the moment of decision; it is their signature moment and sets them apart.

The four cornerstones of leadership; influence, relationships, communication and resolution, have one common denominator. That is effective listening.

## Learn to Listen

Managers and Motivators must learn to listen. Nothing messes up the human relationship more than the lack of communication. We do not like it when we are made to feel that no one is interested in what we've got to say. We do not like it when we are made to feel we are not important enough to be kept up on things. We don't like it because it demeans us, and more importantly, it demotivates us. As managers, our most imperative responsibility is to create the perception we are motivating agents in the efforts and purposes of our people—that we want them to succeed, to be successful. That is what produces the highest form of motivation.

Motivation is based on communication. Communication is based on aggressive, effective listening, which means we convince people who are speaking to us that we are attempting to grasp their entire message. We are not just *hearing their words*, we are *listening to their ideas, thoughts, and emotions* attached to those words. Managers who wish to become *aggressive, effective listeners* must catch the meaning of the words as well as the meaning communicated in nonverbal signals.

Day in and day out, the most important relationship in the lives of workers is their relationship with their immediate supervisor. They want leaders who care and are reliable. Workers yearn for caring leadership that provides reliability, security, and significance, things that are best provided through relationships. Caring and reliability are the characteristics that provide security and significance, and as we are going to see, listening provides us many opportunities to manifest these two characteristics.

The most universal compliments you hear about listeners are "I like so and so; she listens to you" or "You can talk to him." Surveys asking to rate relationship factors in order of influence have consistently come up with the following results:

- Sincere appreciation of work well done
- The feeling of "being in on things"
- Empathetic help on personal problems

All three of these factors are based on superior listening skills. Developing these skills requires work, concentration, and practice.

# TALK #9
# How to Become an Effective, Aggressive Listener

Effective listening is a very demanding behavior. People are very good at camouflaging our feelings and thoughts with our words. A good listener can understand messages being communicated through means other than just words. Unfortunately, we are a nation of poor listeners. Approximately 55% of our communication time is split between speaking, reading, and writing, but 45% is in listening alone. We receive considerable instruction during our school years in reading, writing, and speech but little or none in listening. And yet, listening is our most important communicative skill. The quality and efficiency of communication are significantly improved when we understand the attitudes, opinions, ideas, and suggestions of others. This can only be accomplished by good listening skills.

Now let's discuss the skills we can cultivate that will enable us to avoid the pitfalls that lead to poor listening. Listening demands work, concentration and practice. The first and most important skill that cures poor listening is concentration. Human performance is directly related to concentration: the higher the level of concentration, the higher the level of performance.

## Skill #1: Concentrate

Concentrate, concentrate, concentrate! If you do not concentrate at the moment of implementation, you will not implement correctly or effectively. This rule applies to any human endeavor or performance, but it is especially true for listening.

I am going to take you into the world of sports to illustrate this point and then relate it to listening. In football, your wide receivers are so-called because they position themselves away from the rest of the offensive formation. They don't want anyone bugging them. They just want to get open, catch the pass and make the big play. During the week, they practice routes, and patterns within those routes, read the defense, get in the open and catch the pass. During the week, all goes well. But Sunday is different. On Sunday, when he goes up for the pass, he hears footsteps that belong to a defensive halfback, the most vicious hitter on the field, intent on sending a message, "don't catch passes in my area of the field!" If the wide receiver, when he goes up for the ball, listens to those footsteps, he will drop the ball because his concentration is broken. But when he makes a catch despite the footsteps, the announcer says, "Look at that concentration."

Now you may think, that was a nice dissertation on football, but what's it got to do with listening? It's got everything to do with listening. Every time we try to listen, there's a defensive halfback on our tail. Where? Our defensive halfback is that voice in our subconscious that never shuts up. Remember those times when you've been talking to someone, and then you walk away, and someone asks you, "What were you talking about?" And you end up saying, "Hell, I don't know." And the reason you don't know is that you were listening to that defensive halfback when the person was talking to you. In the world of listening, it is called self-talk. We always talk to ourselves; that's whom we talk to the most. When we drive, eat, sleep and, unfortunately, when talking to others, we self-talk. And we never stop unless we really work at not doing it. Self-talk is much faster than what we're listening to. When agitated or excited, the rate at which you self-talk jumps even more.

## Skill #2: No Multiple Conversations

You can hear a number of people at one time, but you cannot intelligently listen to more than one conversation at one time. Hearing is our natural response to sound. Our eardrums involuntarily vibrate. This is a physical response requiring no engagement from you. (For example, you can hear the television is on or that your spouse is talking). Listening is the willful attempt to understand conceptually. It is mental, emotional, and purposeful.

## Skill #3: Do Not Interrupt

If you remember nothing else, remember this one. The worst of the listening sins, one we commit the most, is interrupting, and you cannot become any kind of an effective listener if you interrupt. One of the things going on when we interrupt is our self-talk. We jump to our own conclusion.

How do you feel when interrupted? Maybe angry, frustrated. What do you think of the interrupter? Rude, selfish, arrogant. What would you like to do to the interrupter? This is what we make others feel when we interrupt. It is not influential.

## Skill #4: Stop Talking

Who is going to win, talking or listening? It takes three years to learn to talk and the rest of our lives learning to shut up. Vince Lombardi said, "The best way to show your mastery of the English language is to say nothing." Your ears will never cause you to lose your job, but your mouth will. The more you listen, the better you sound. Lincoln said, "It's better to say nothing and be thought a fool than to open your mouth and remove all doubt." Speak less, listen more.

How we feel about yakkers (by which I mean people who can't stop talking) is a philosophical question. At a party, a yakker walks towards you; you turn, make sure there is no eye contact, and hope they don't come to you. Or in another instance, it's a beautiful day, great agenda, getting things done, then the phone rings and . . . it's one of them. The message to all of us is that when you talk too long, what you're saying becomes less meaningful and less effective.

## Skill #5: Be Interested

We must convince the person speaking that we are listening to them. Now we are going to add a subtle requirement. Convince me you want to listen to me, and then I'll believe you "are" listening to me. You do this through external behaviors of establishing eye contact, body positioning, and appropriate facial expression. It's also necessary to remove distractions. Turn off your phone, shut the door, and hold all of your calls.

## Skill #6: Don't Have Time? Say So.

Don't continue doing what you were doing, and act as if you're listening. This is demeaning to the person who needs to speak with you. It says that what you're doing is more important than what I have to say. If you can't stop, say so and tell them you'll get to them and do it. Keep your word.

## Skill #7: What Over Who

Be influenced by what is being said, not by who is saying it. We don't like to admit to this one because it's based on prejudice and bias. This is not just racial, ethical, or gender-related. Many good ideas are lost because the person presenting them is someone we don't like. We might not like the way they talk, walk, or dress. We don't like their hair, or whatever, so we don't listen to them. We are all prejudiced to some degree in some area. That's not the problem. The problem is that we deny it. We don't have to deal with something we don't do. To deny the problem is to deny the solution. To handle and deal with your prejudice, you must first admit it.

## Skill #8: Hear What is Being Said, Not What You Want to Hear

Since creation, man has always attempted to reduce truth to a subjective experience or personal opinion. We like to manufacture truth. For example, observe how people treat the Bible or the text of the U.S. Constitution. This is a constant source of misunderstanding because we subtract or add to what is being said until it conforms to what we want it to be. The emotion that creates most of our problems in this area is enthusiasm. When we are enthusiastic about anything, we are looking for agreement, not opinion, and we impose rather than expose our ideas. This can cause you to lose good input.

## Skill #9: Responsibilities of the Listener

Meet the responsibilities of the listener. When we seek support or need to unload, we don't call a motor mouth. We call a listener. Adhere to the listener's code:

- Never minimize a person's problems by exaggerating your own. (Husbands, when wives are expressing some frustration, the last thing they want to hear is what you would have done. Listen.)
- Limit yourself to your capabilities and training. (Some people reduce alcohol and drugs to moral and educational issues. They are addictions)
- Maintain confidentiality. (The surest way to destroy a relationship is to share something told to you in confidence)

## Highlights that bear repeating

- When you listen, you make others feel interesting, intelligent, and important.
- Concentrate! Concentrate! Concentrate!
- The more you listen, the better you sound.
- If you're consistently too busy to listen, you're too busy.

- Admit your prejudices and your enthusiasm.
- There is no change without changing, so pick out what you need to work on and start *right now!*

# TALK #10
# The Productive Personality Straight A's

We all want that straight "A" report card of being *accepted, appreciated, admired,* and *advanced,* but we often forget that such a report card demands work. Youngsters must be taught that they must help others to want to give them what they want; that people do not respond graciously to their demands or attitude of entitlement. Youngsters must come to understand that adults respond to them based on how they behave. In other words, you can't act like an "ass" and expect to be treated like a "face."

**Distinguishing Actions**

These are the actions we can teach young people to take that will help them get the desired A's.

- **Personal Appearance:** It's the first impression we make. When applying for a job, you do not get a second chance to make a first impression. Clothes don't make you but they do introduce you.
- **Politeness:** Politeness is to the human being what heat is to wax: It melts you. Manners used to be part of our school's curriculum. It should be reinstated. Kids are not polite. Rude is cool.
- **Punctuality:** We do not like people who are late. Use the

five-minute rule: if you can't be on time, be five minutes early!
- **Promptness:** Don't procrastinate. Do what you're supposed to do first. ASAP. Freedom is gained by doing what you ought to do, not what you want to do.
- **Perseverance:** Never, never, never give up. Do not be seduced by the doctrine of easy, quick, convenient and comfortable. Remember that quitters never win, and winners never quit. A great example of perseverance is the life story of Abe Lincoln. He went bankrupt twice, had two nervous breakdowns, lost a son and a brother, lost seven elections and then became President of the United States.
- **Pride:** Do what needs to be done, not for the admiration of others, but for one's own self-worth. Many desire to succeed but only a few desire to prepare to succeed.

We must seek to continually grow the above listed habits of action through constant self-assessment. Say to yourself, "I'm good today, but I'll be better tomorrow." If any of you think you're as good as you're ever going to be, you are on your way down. That's the law of nature. As soon as any living organism stops growing, it immediately starts dying. You must constantly self-assess to continually grow.

Do not confuse self-assessment and evaluation. Evaluations are based on calendar and policy. They are an "event." By contrast, self-assessment is based on motivation and performance. It is a process. These skills produce the productive person.

***"Reputation is precious and is what others believe about you. Character is priceless and is what you know about yourself."***

# TALK #11
# Motivation

Let's first distinguish between *motivated* and *motivational*. Motivated means you know what you want, know what to do, and you do it. You have passion for what you want. Motivational means you are all of the above (motivated), but you also purposefully encourage and give others the opportunity to succeed. You have passion for what you want and compassion for what others want.

Successful leaders create the perception that they are motivating agents in the efforts of others; that they want others to be successful. Convincing others that you want them to succeed is the key to their minds and hearts. Successful leaders not only try to meet the demands of the organization, they also attempt to fulfill the needs of the people.

With these thoughts in mind, we will start our discussion on behaviors that are motivational and develop relationships. Relationships are everything in the human experience. Relationships are a process, not an event. The relationship process demands time and energy. Invest in people.

## Strategies of a Motivational Person

From this point on, we will discuss strategies that cause others to see you as a motivational person, that you want more for them than you do for yourself.

**Delegation**

Delegation is a concept that most people accept intellectually but not emotionally. Why not? Simply put, once we establish domain and power, we do not want to share it. This works directly against the notion of empowerment which is just the opposite. It is based on the sharing of productivity, responsibility, and authority. The usual excuse for not delegating is, "If I don't do it myself, it won't get done right. I've got to do it all myself."

Delegation is not only *motivational*; it is *inspirational* because it fulfills three inspiring attitudes in your people. One, it raises the person to whom you delegate to a higher level of function. He can feel, "The leader is aware of me." (do not confuse this with "Task Assignment.") Next, it increases the person's range and degree of responsibility. He thinks, "The leader has confidence in me." Third, it expands the person's base of authority. It implies, "The leader trusts me."

This empowers, uplifts, and inspires people. In street talk, delegation means putting your money where your mouth is. Delegation manifests and demonstrates what you believe which is more convincing than just *saying what you believe*. Delegation bridges the gap between belief and faith. Belief is intellectual; faith is actual. When you show faith in others, it increases their faith in themselves.

*Guidelines for delegating*
- Before delegating, be certain the person to whom you are delegating can accomplish the goal. Make sure the individual knows, understands and is capable.
- Correct mistakes immediately. Discuss what went wrong, then teach the best way to handle it.
- Recognize and praise accomplishments as soon as possible. If you do this, you will never hear the common lament from your people: "Do ten things right, and you never hear a word. Do one thing wrong, and you never hear the end of it."

## Unshared or Undivided Attention

No drive influences the development of the human personality more than the drive for individuality and uniqueness. Our hair, clothes, cars, homes, jewelry, et cetera each show our strong desire to be unique and special. As a result, it is extremely important to give others individual and personal attention. This is what shows that you value and care about them. *This is very important!*

When giving unshared attention, be prepared to discuss specific and personal matters. For example, you may talk to a person about his or her value and importance to you and the organization; a service he or she performed; a friend he or she helped; a family crisis he or she has faced. This kind of conversation is what conveys individuality and uniqueness and causes your people to feel secure, significant, and irreplaceable. It shows you know them and are aware of them. Never relegate these moments to small talk or irrelevant matters. When these moments are well spent they pay huge dividends over the long haul.

## Patience

The Apostle Paul wrote that "Love is patient." Patience is your behavior when you are waiting. Another way of describing a leader's patience could be power under control.

Perseverance is the foremost trait of leadership, and patience is the cornerstone of perseverance. We are not born patient. Patience is an ability that must be learned and practiced forever. To be a motivational individual, you must be patient. The best way to approach this topic is to compare the positive results of patience versus the negative consequence of impatience.

*Patience Produces Security*

The patient person makes you feel worthy and accepted for who you are. Patience understands we are not the same, nor are we equally gifted.

*Willingness to try;* The patient person frees you from

the fear of challenge, freeing you to make the attempt because patience allows for mistakes.

*Trust;* The patient person convinces you that they want you to succeed. We trust people who enable and encourage our success. As Steven R. Covey is credited with saying, "Trust is the highest form of motivation."

*Communication;* The patient person is a good listener. He fulfills our need for self-respect. When others show interest in what we've got to say, it makes us feel we are important. And communication from you shows you believe your people are worthy of that respect.

*Impatience Produces Insecurity*

Impatience, initmidation, poor listening, dissimissiveness, demeaning questions and overbearing control by the leaders causes a lack of trust, communication and creativity which leads to hositility and insecurity.

**"The patient person conveys security and significance
The impatient person projects control and arrogance."**

## Praise and Recognition

Maslow tells us that the only human need that can never be satisfied is praise and recognition. As a result, the most significant factor in motivation is praise and recognition. To see an illustration of this principle, consider rich, successful people who don't need money but will perform in difficult, demanding situations. Why do they do it? Because they still need the inspirational love of their fans or audiences. Praise and Recognition are the only human needs that can never be satisfied.

Praise is the art of catching others doing well and serves two purposes. First, it reassures us. To some degree, we all worry and are anxious about our performance and our responsibilities. Praise alleviates that tension.

It also makes us feel good. It's good to feel good. When

we feel good, we tend to say and do good things. When we feel bad, we tend to say and do bad things.

Remember the power of the tongue. A mere comment can be uplifting or devastating, and the finest gifts we can give one another are free. It costs nothing to smile or give a compliment. For example, you go to work feeling great, and a coworker tells you that you look beat. The rest of the day, you are! Or you picked up a skirt at the resale shop, and you're feeling great. A co-worker says, "Hey, I gave a skirt away like that the other day." In both cases, the careless comments induced anxiety and made someone feel bad.

## Be the Example

Live what you profess and earn the right to demand of others, not through your position, but rather through your own behavior. Model what you want others to see and to be. Never forget that people do not see or remember what you say; they see and remember what you do. For a Christian, this is what we mean when we say, "We are in Christ." Being in Christ is not merely mental assent; it must manifest itself in the physical world of action. People cannot read your mind, but they can read your actions. The light on the hill is a physical reality that can be seen.

# TALK #12
# Obligations of Managers and Supervisors

Organizations and employees have reciprocal obligations. The obligation of the organization to the employee is to clearly spell out basic tasks and performance requirements of the job, and to provide salary, benefits, resources and opportunities. The obligation of the employee of the organization is to do whatever is necessary to get the job done, and in the process demonstrate trust and loyalty to the organization. These obligations define our relationship and are the basis for our expectations.

## Developing Your Organization's Most Valuable Asset

What does a human being want? I posit that a person's desires fit into four categories:

***Physical***: People want existence and living. This is our physical area. Self-preservation and survival are our two strongest drives. We want to exist, but more than that, we want to live. We want the necessities, but we also seek the comforts and conveniences. We seek pleasure and avoid pain. We want rewards for our efforts and ownership of our material reality.

***Emotional:*** The Bible teaches that these remain: "Faith,

Hope, and Love, but the greatest of these is love." This is our emotional area. We are ordained to love and be loved; to belong. Relationships are our everything. We want another to reach out. We want the security of care, patience, kindness, joyfulness, and goodness. We want to feel we are trustworthy and have self-respect and self-esteem. We want to be important in the lives of our significant others.

***Mental:*** Development, Independence, Dreams. This is our mental area. We want to achieve, and we want the status that goes with that achievement. We want to be used productively and qualitatively. And we especially want ownership of our special ideas.

***Spiritual:*** Impact, Difference, Contributions. We want to linger. This is our spiritual area. We want to feel we've left something after we're gone; that we were significant and really mattered. We need to feel there was purpose and meaning to our lives and that, in some way, we are irreplaceable.

People make choices. They choose and decide how much they give of themselves to their work, and that choice will depend on the opportunity they are given to fulfill the four parts of their nature. *The worker who is...*
- paid fairly
- treated with care
- used productively and specially
- enabled to serve others in fulfilling ways

*...will become your most valuable asset.*

## Management

As part of the leadership of your organization you must know how and when to wear two hats. The hat of *management* and the hat of *leadership*.

The management hat is defined and delegated by the

organization. The function of this hat is to serve the organization by maintaining and implementing policies and procedures. The purpose of the management hat is to produce predictable and productive behavior and present the organization in its' best light. The management hat is based on the power of the authority delegated by the organization. When you wear this hat, you take few, if any, risks.

## Suggestions to Management
- *Hire Well:* If you start with poor material you end up with a poor product.
- *Train Well:* If you want people to do the job the way you want it done, invest the time and money to train them.
- *Pay Well*: If you hire well and train well, you will want to keep your people. In order to do that, you need to pay them. Always remember that people stay where they are appreciated and money speaks your appreciation.

## Leading as a Supervisor
Supervisors observe, direct and redirect behavior. While the management hat is defined by the organization, the leadership hat is defined by your personal capabilities and performance. Its main function is to provide direction and response to change and to develop the desire and capacity for creativity. The purpose of the leadership hat is to allow the pursuit of possibilities and participation. The leadership hat is based on your capacity to influence people. As a leader, you must take risks.

## Suggestions to Supervisors
- *Know Your Job*: The security of your staff is based upon the perception that they "are in good hands."
- *Be the Example*: Your ability to lead is absolutely based upon this quality. Walk your talk.
- *Talk Common Sense*: Fancy jargon and theory turn people off. They recognize the seminar/workshop syndrome. Talk real about real things.

- *Be Fair*: Nothing commands respect more than fairness, and nothing commands disrespect more than unfairness. Beware of your prejudices.
- *Evaluate*: Use evaluations to evaluate, not to build morale, relationships, punish, or to avoid confrontation. Evaluations not based on performance will come back to haunt you!
- *Keep Improving*: "I'm good today, but I'll be better tomorrow." This takes constant self-assessment.
- *Be a Developer*: The most reasonable and efficient manner to increase productivity is developing people. Give them proper assignments and make certain they know, understand, and are capable of carrying out those assignments.
- *Be a Leader*: Know what you want and convince others to do it. Be ready and willing to delegate, re-arrange, and eliminate. Always remember your staff is constantly observing you and they are extremely aware of your attitudes, behavior and relationship style. Your ability to wear both the management and leadership hats determines your worth to the organization and staff.

# TALK #13
# Two Common Difficulties Leaders Face

**How a Leader Manages Change**
Someone once said, "You can never cross the same river twice." Change is a constant in life. It bothers and threatens us because it demands adjustment. We want to hold on to the comforts, gains and routines we already have. We tend to perceive change as depriving us of these advantages. Change, including change in structure, duties, people, superiors, and technology, is a chief cause of stress in the workplace. It is natural for people to resist change. Let's discuss a few principles that reduce that resistance.

*Communicate*
Inform staff ASAP of oncoming changes. Be clear and honest. Give the reasons for the change. Share with them what they stand to lose or gain. Trust increases when truth is shared and makes it easier for people to handle their feelings.

Involve everyone. Encourage discussion, and solicit views, criticisms and possible solutions. Be available and keep an open dialogue through the entire process of planning and implementation. Give your team new information and listen to their feedback. As much as possible, do this communication person to person.

*Use Patience*

Go slow and give people time to adjust. It takes time to see the results of change. Don't force conclusions based on your enthusiasm. Allow people to make up their own minds.

*Praise and Recognize*

Recognize the efforts of people. Acknowledge their struggles and contributions. Praise them.

## How a Leader Manages the Difficult Employee

Let's start this discussion by distinguishing between *bad* and *difficult*. Bad is measured by policies, procedures, job descriptions, and documentation and is handled through the formal disciplinary process that is applied to everyone. Bad is measured by objective standards. By contrast, difficult is not so easily defined or managed. It is perceived in terms of attitude, habits, personality, bias, et cetera, and must be handled at the personal level in a manner applicable to the individual. As a result, *difficult* is quite often measured by subjective standards.

Because of its subjective nature, a prudent first step is to determine whether or not a personality conflict is at the root of the problem. Look for indicators that can help you make this determination, such as:
- You are unusually indifferent or hostile.
- You are less effective than usual in handling their behavior.
- Others have significantly different feelings and experiences with the same employee.

Regardless of whether the difficulty is limited to you or widespread, constructive action must be initiated. The following are a few suggestions you may find helpful:
- Describe and present specific problems.
- Seek and listen to their side of the story.

- Summarize both sides.
- Discuss reciprocal strategies for resolution.
- Involve others who can contribute to the improvement of the situation.
- Schedule a regular meeting time for re-statement and evaluation of progress.

***"When you succeed in helping a difficult individual to turn around, you usually end up with one of your best and most loyal employees."***

# TALK #14
# The Destroyer: Stress

Stress destroys relationships. Stress will destroy you. It is the greatest of all killers. Stress is the physical and emotional exhaustion that occurs when we are convinced that we do not have the ability or resources to deal with our problems. We are overwhelmed. When you are being pressed, stress is your reaction to the pressure.

There are many adverse outcomes caused by mismanaged stress. These include migraines, heart disease, stomach and intestinal problems, pain, and other health problems. Most importantly, stress weakens our immune system. The tremendous use of alcohol, tranquilizers, and a variety of other drugs as well as suicides are linked to stress. Stress can even cause death. Stress is often cited as a contributing factor to sudden cardiac deaths each year.

We can adjust our external behaviors to reduce the effects of stress on our lives. Here are 7 behaviors to avoid being destroyed by stress.

- *Just say no:* The best labor-saving device ever invented is to learn to say no. Without this, you will pervasively over-promise, over-schedule and over-commit which leads to stress.
- *Set priorities:* Stay in control. Make lists and prioritize them. Stress-free is doing what you ought to do, not what

you want to do. *Do not procrastinate.* Procrastination makes you always behind in tasks and always in a hurry. Never leaving enough time guarantees stress.
- *Delegate:* Doing everything yourself does not give you power. It gives you ulcers. If you do it all yourself, you make others hostile. They think, "He has to do it all himself" and "She doesn't trust." Instead, share, share, share the load!
- *Help others:* It is literally impossible for you to help someone else feel good without you feeling better. Call someone and tell them you appreciate them. Help others, and you help yourself. This is Christ's principle of duplication: Give to others, and you give to yourself. When you die, the only thing you take with you is what you have given to others.
- *Choose and control your attitudes*: Do not tolerate moods. Human energy is neutral. What happens to you is often not your choice, but how you react to it is. Do not load your mood onto others.
- *Find the humor:* Laugh, laugh, and laugh some more. Laughter releases health-enhancing chemicals in our body, making stress much more manageable. Laugh with, not at, others.
- *Choose a confidante:* This is someone with whom you can share and *trust*; someone you can unload to and get things off your chest; one who can bring a different perspective. You must not be too prideful to seek help. Seek mentors who are successful and can help you grow. Confide to God; he is always there. God and you make a majority.

# Common Sense about Christian Life

"To be the salt and light; which is an exciting, interesting, encouraging follower of Christ, you must be reliable, accountable, and willing" N.S.

# TALK #15
# The Responsible Christian

We're going to discuss an important human function: responsibility. I stress *human* because we are the only ones of God's creatures who are not governed by instinct. We have intelligence and free will. As a result, we are the only creatures who can be responsible and be held responsible.

Early in his ministry, Christ said, "I want you to be the Salt and the Light of this world." What did He mean? The best way to answer that question is to define His metaphors. Salt is tasty, zesty, and tangy, is a preservative, and increases the flavor of any food it touches. Light brushes back darkness, allowing us to enjoy sight. Salt and Light are attractive and enjoyable. Our Lord's message is simple and direct. "That's what I want you to be." Exciting, fun, joyful, interesting, considerate, and encouraging. I do not want you to be sour, dour, and judgmental. Christ wants followers who are attractive, who in turn will attract and influence others. He wants followers who shine brightly in their behavior and their character. He wants followers who stand out and who are outstanding.

What is the most attractive, outstanding human characteristic? In my opinion, I believe it to be responsibility. Responsibility is universally admired. Winston Churchill stated it beautifully when he said, "The price of greatness is responsibility." The whole world loves the responsible person. Christ wants us to be responsible Christians and be attractive to the whole world.

## Reliability

At this point, it behooves us to identify the traits of a responsible Christian. Reliability occupies the top position. Reliability is so attractive. It simply means "keep your word." Do what you say you are going to do; be trustworthy. Christ teaches this in a very strong and direct manner when He tells us, "Let your yes be your yes and your no be your no." He ends this verse with the very terse statement "anything beyond this comes from the evil one - *Matthew 5:37-39*." Christ is telling us to live transparently and purely so that our simplest statements are easily accepted as valid by our pledge to our faith and our character. It is a rather stern statement, and Christ intended it to be so. He was teaching the importance of reliability.

Reliability is the mother of trust, and trust is the cornerstone of all human relationships. We do not relate to people who are devoid of trust. Ask yourself how do you feel about someone you do not trust? Do you like them? Do you want them around you? If you are unreliable, you will not be the attractive Salt or Light Christ wants you to be. We teach reliability by emphasizing the keeping of your word! Integrity is keeping your word.

We are all born self-centered and thoughtless. Babies soon reduce the English language to two words: "Mine and No." We are not born responsible, we are born with the capacity to be responsible. It is a learned function, and as such, responsibility must be taught, learned, and practiced: taught by adults, learned by kids, and practiced by both, especially the adult. Example is the only way to teach behavior. Your example earns you the moral right to demand. Example earns you the right to exert the authority of your position.

## Accountability

The second important character trait of the responsible Christian is accountability. Accountability is the quality of taking ownership of your own actions. Accountability projects honesty. Do not rationalize and project your behavior all over the place by trying to justify your wrongs or trying to blame everybody else for them.

**Accountability in the Bible**

Look up *Genesis 3:12-13* and scrutinize it through the lens of accountability. Who, Adam, Eve or the Serpent, is rationalizing their behavior, justifying their decisions or taking ownership of their actions? In *Matthew 25:14-30*, Jesus relates the Parable of the Talents. Consider what this teaching of our Lord adds to the discussion of accountability.

Our world is filled with this today. No one is accountable; everybody is a victim. God does not accept unaccountability. It is dishonest. People are repelled by dishonesty. We don't like it. Accountability is the mother of honesty. God gave us His A's formula for accountability:

- Admit: confess your actions
- Apologize: be remorseful and seek forgiveness
- Accept: suffer the consequences of your behavior
- Advance: repent and move on. David did not become a man of God until he accepted accountability.

**Willingness**

The third trait of the responsible Christian is willingness. Christians should desire to share the burden and help carry the load. Instead of making excuses for why they can't, they always offer any help they can. They should constantly project the idea that the best way to serve God is to serve others.

Willingness is the mother of appreciation. The willing Christian finds joy and thankfulness for what God has provided. They improve and increase the value of whatever situation in which they find themselves. The willing Christian lives by the motto, "If you want more for others than you want for yourself, you will never want."

**Willingness in Scriptures**
*Proverbs 11:25* "He who refreshes others will himself be refreshed." *Proverbs 11:27* "He who seeks good finds goodwill." *Romans 12:6-8* "If it is serving, let him serve; if it is teaching, let him teach; . . . if it is leadership, let him govern diligently."

**Responsibility**
Responsibility is the centerpiece between God and man. God could not punish or reward man if we did not possess the capacity to be responsible. What difference would it make if an action were right or wrong if we could not be responsible for that difference? God in His perfect justice would have to ignore it.

What happens when responsibility is not given its due? Standards of language, manners and dress have been shattered. Kids are under-disciplined, under-supervised, and under-socialized. They are bored. Boredom is too much privilege and not enough responsibility.

To be the salt and light; which is an exciting, interesting and encouraging follower of Christ, you must be reliable, accountable, and willing.

My Role Model in the Scriptures would have to be Paul.
- He was Reliable almost to extinction.
- He was Accountable in all things to his death.
- He was Willing to the last drop and beyond.
- He became the single most important human in Christian History.
- He attracted and influenced nations.

# TALK #16
# Christians as Role Models, Christian Obedience

**Role Model**

Did Christ place importance on example? The fact that one of the first of Christ's command teachings is on the importance of example illustrates the emphasis and necessity He places on it.

**Bible Verses about Example**
- *Matthew 5:14-16:* Jesus compares his followers to a light shining before others. He re-emphasizes the need for this quality many times over in His teachings. Let's examine this teaching to better understand its importance in relationship to God, to others and to ourselves.
- *Titus 2:7-8:* Christians are to set an example; the example of our behavior impacts others.
- *1 Timothy 4:11-12:* The expectation that a role model should do more than, better than, and more consistently than that which he demands of others.
- *Matthew 7:21-23:* It is not enough for the role model to simply do the right thing. The goal of a role model is to teach the right thing to do and to do it for the right reason.
- *Matthew 20:25-28:* What does being a good example

earn for you? It earns you the right to demand. Position gives you the authority to demand. Example earns you the right to exert that authority.

Many Christians carry a burden of guilt that causes them to feel they are not capable or worthy of being role models. They fail to realize that one of the greatest gifts of grace is the opportunity we have to repent. Paul tells us to not look back. God does not use the past to forge our future. Moses was a murderer, David was an adulterer and murderer, and Paul pursued Christians and participated in the killing of Stephen. These three individuals confessed, repented, made their peace with God and moved on to become three great men of God. With God, nothing is impossible, so don't try to tell Him what can or cannot be done.

Being a constant role model is difficult and hard work. It demands focus and intensity. Merely being interested in being an example is not sufficient. Intensity is the key. Interest creates the desire to be; intensity creates the power to be. And you must stay focused because once you are identified and marked as an example of goodness, you are put under a magnifying glass.

In His teachings Christ constantly emphasizes that the price of greatness is setting the example.

## The Beauty of Obedience

Disobedience is pervasive in man and causes him most of his problems. The biblical demonstrations of this fact include the stories of Adam and Eve, Moses, Samson, Saul and more. The most essential task of leadership is knowing how to elicit obedience from others. In the Christian ethic, leadership should be through servanthood. See *Matthew 20:25-28* and *Luke 22:25-28*.

Structure, order, coherence and beauty all flow from obedience. Balance is absolutely based upon it. Without obedience, there is no harmony. Without harmony, none of the above will happen. To be effective in teaching children to obey, we must be obedient in our own lives. The greatest lack in the lives of children today is the lack of healthy role models. Don't expect them to do what you don't do. Discipline and Consequences are the twin towers of obedience. They must be built upon the cornerstones of role modeling, policy, and philosophy.

## The Nature of Obedience

The essential nature of obedience is stressed by God throughout Scripture:
- *Genesis 22:18* "And through your offspring all nations on the earth will be blessed because you have obeyed me."
- *Leviticus 18:4-5* "You must obey my laws and be careful to follow my decrees. I am the Lord your God. Keep my decrees and laws, for the man who obeys them will live by them. I am the Lord." Note: Obedience means you incorporate the laws into your daily life (work, home, community), not just lip service, but with your heart.
- *Psalm 119:4* "You have laid down precepts that are to be fully obeyed."
- *Proverbs 19:16* "He who obeys instructions guards his life, but he who is contemptuous of his ways will die."
- *Micah 5:15* "I will take vengeance in anger and wrath upon the nations that have not obeyed me."
- *John 14:15* "If you love me, obey my commands."
- *John 14:21* "Whoever has my commands and obeys them, he is the one who loves me."
- *John 14:23* "If anyone loves me, he will obey my teachings."
- *I John 2:3-4* "We know we have come to know him if we obey his commands. The man who says, "I know him," but does not do what He commands is a liar, and the truth is not in him."

**Definitions of Terms**
- *Discipline:* Consistent enforcement of one's standards. *Proverbs 10:17, 12:1, 13:18, 13:24, 22:15*
- *Consequences:* A result of an action. These must be immediate and meaningful in order to be effective. Delayed punishment leads to more wrongdoing. *Ecclesiastes 8:11*
- *Role Modeling:* Do more than, better than and more consistently than what you demand. Follow the teachings of Christ!
- *Policy:* Make certain others know, understand, and are capable of doing what you expect. Christ used parables.
- *Philosophy:* Your ultimate responsibility is to do your best to give others the opportunity to make the right choice. *Matthew 10:14-15, Luke 9:4-5*

# TALK #17
# Do Not Judge

*"We judge so we can blame. We judge so we can perfect ourselves through the imperfections of others."*

Christ knows we are naturally inclined towards this type of behavior. He also knows no human organization—family, workplace, church, et cetera— can survive it.

Christ emphatically commands, "Do not judge others" *Matthew 7:1-5*. To be clear on what Christ is saying, we must distinguish between the judgment of discerning and the judgment of condemning. He is not saying we are not to discern right from wrong. If we read *Matthew 18:15-17*, Christ gives the example of discerning judgment, which implies the identification of the problem, discussion, and solution. We are repeatedly told to use discerning judgment; see *1 Thessalonians 5:21-22* for another example.

**Discerning Judgement**

Discerning judgment is the correction for the future. Christ is addressing condemnatory judgment. This judgment demands the determination of guilt, condemnation, and punishment. It is the just and necessary function of governing bodies such as the state, the military and church leadership to use for the collective good, see *Romans 13:1-7*. By contrast, individual Christians are not to use condemnatory judgment in personal relationships, see *1 Corinthians*

*4:4-6, Romans 2:1, and Proverbs 3:5.*

## Condemenatory Judgement

Condemnatory judgment is for the past. The message of Christ is to show mercy and grace to others. According to *James 2:12-13*, the way we judge others is the way he will judge us. Christ gives us examples to follow: Peter, Thomas, and Woman at the well, but his defining example was the adulteress in *John 8:1-11*. Here Christ establishes the absolute principle that only a perfectly guiltless person has the right to judge another person. He was the only such person to live, but He chose to discern and resolve rather than condemn and punish. He does not ignore her behavior. He tells her to go and sin no more. He chose mercy rather than punishment. Christ told us we are the sowers, and He is the reaper. He warns us not to try to be both.

# TALK #18
# Be Patient

Christ wants us to be motivational people. To be motivational you must be patient. It is contradictory to think you can be impatient and motivational. No one is born patient. It is an ability we must practice and develop. Patience understands we are not all equally gifted.

**Scriptures About Patience**
- *Proverbs 14:29:* "A patient man has great understanding."
- *Proverbs 16:32:* "Better a patient man than a warrior."
- *Thessalonians 5:14:* "Encourage the timid, help the weak, be patient with everyone."
- *2 Timothy 4:2*: "Correct, rebuke, and encourage—with great patience and careful instruction."

Impatient listeners put others down. They can't help saying things like, "Get to the point." "I haven't got all day." "That's not helpful." People lose the desire and confidence to communicate when faced with these impatient responses. They avoid impatient listeners. You can learn!

Patience is the heart and soul feeling of leadership. Patience projects acceptance and worth. There is no gray area. You are either patient or impatient. Patience creates the perception of kindness, empathy, and compassion and says, "I want you to succeed." Finally, patience is a fruit of the Spirit listed in *Galatians 5:22-23*.

## The emotional impact of two leaders

The *patient leader* has an attitude of servant-leadership and conveys love to his people through the following:
- Security: You are somebody. No one wants to feel like a nobody.
- Creativity and Risk-Taking
- Trust and Loyalty: We like people who trust us. We are loyal to them
- Authoritative
- Attentiveness

By contrast, the *impatient leader* affects arrogance and power:
- Fear: We can't bear the impact of their attitude. Impatient leaders are negative, demanding and critical.
- Rigid Conformity: Their demand for conformity makes us hesitant and tentative. We feel we can't do anything right.
- Hostility
- Authoritarian
- Negative Listening: Impatient people convince you they don't want to listen. They don't care about your feelings.
- They are ignoring you.

***"Patient people convince you they have listened to you. They validate your feelings. They did not ignore you. Patience is motivational."***

# The Ending

You can see in these talks that Nick used powerful words, spoke with authority, presented with confidence and truly believed in the material he was presenting. His passion for sharing, performing, educating and caring about the individual before him is worth more words that I can ever write, speak or think to do it justice. There is only one word that I can relate to Nick that would begin to touch the essence of what he was - *Dynamic*. Not used as an adjective but as a noun:

*Dynamic (n) - a force that stimulates change or progress within a system or process. Greek root word - Dunamis (Power)*

To rephrase it - Nick was a force that stimulated change or progress within a system, process, individual or group of individuals. Nick had **Dunamis**, a power that you could feel when he entered the room, when he took the stage, when he listened to you, when he put his arm around you...you knew Nick Seta was there. - Franklin Seta

# Reflections from Nick's Friends and Family

## Note from Nick's daughter Andrea

**Dear Dad, It takes a great man to build successfully what you built. It will never be done again for a greater man than you will never be. I love you. Andrea   CUS 1970**

## Stephen Seta, Nick's son

Although I could pick many, one moment embodies best my thoughts on who was Nick Seta. Walking downtown, I'm maybe 12 at the time, we encountered a homeless man yelling his name: "Mr. Seta! Mr. Seta!" Nick immediately knew who it was—one of his kids grown up from his time at Longview State Hospital. The man asked about a shirt Nick had promised him, but Nick had forgotten the shirt. Well, he promptly took the shirt off his back and gave it to the man. We walked the rest of the time downtown and all he had on from his pants up was his sport coat. That's Nick Seta—he'd literally give you the shirt off his back. His word meant everything and to break it would make him nothing.

A true giver who never met a stranger.
Philosophically sound and true to his faith while foregoing the judgment of others.
A counselor to the high and low alike.
A teacher of teachers and a motivator to the masses.
An imperfect man with a perfect heart.
May we all find a way to be a little more like him.

## Maria Jackson, Nick's Daughter

My dad always said, "Do what you're supposed to do first." Not say, not feel, not think...DO. When we do what we're supposed to do, our thoughts and feelings will follow. My dad understood this more than anyone. Yes, "doing what you're supposed to do first" also suggests self-discipline, self-motivation, and responsibility for ourselves. He felt these characteristics were important.

Doing what you're supposed to do first, means doing it when you're tired, sad, angry, resentful, confused, and maybe even broken. What my dad knew is that if we have trained ourselves to do what we are supposed to do first, we have a better chance of making it out of whatever difficult time we are in. What people see as strength, resilience, or determination is really just me "doing what I'm supposed to do first."

We all know those things we are supposed to be doing first. It could mean making your bed, doing your homework, taking a shower, spending time with a friend in need, praying, cooking, going to work, etc. Doing what you're supposed to do first never impacted my individualism and it wasn't confining or strict. He never said don't have fun doing what you're supposed to do. My dad wanted me to live right. My parents taught me discernment so that I could be myself and have fun while doing what I was supposed to do first and spreading the love of Christ.

## John Carmen Seta, Nick's cousin

When I was a young Italian kid, always hearing about my cousin and his accomplishments, Nick grew to be an icon in my mind. I watched him from afar for quite a few years. His son Nick and I were both born in 1948, I in the month of July and Nicky in the month of August. Nicky and I hung for a short while when Nick and Birdie lived in Mt. Auburn on Burnet Avenue.

When Nick would attend an Italian event, we all would take notice because of his energy. He would give you a hearty tag on your chest and would make some sly comment that would intimidate you. Despite feeling intimidated, you enjoyed the brief encounter! You wanted more of his presence. When Nick was around, I kept my eye on him as he communicated with all the Italian men of our community. He had this draw and command from the Italian community and for me. I was aware of his commanding appearance and his words.

My relationship with Nick grew over the years, especially after the death of his son Nicky. We would, from time to time, run into each other. When I lived in Finneytown for a short stint, I connected with Birdie and the girls. I would see Nick at my Uncle Don's house where my grandfather was living and through our conversations, we built a slow but meaningful relationship over time.

I recall one conversation we had over a lunch at Maggiano's. We were discussing our spiritual commitment to God. I said, "I believe in God." Nick's comment was, "I'm happy that you do, but do you *believe* God." Nick's comment has stuck with me to this very day. I often use it when folks make the same comment to me. "I believe in God" they say. When I ask, "Do you *believe* God," I see the same bewilderment I felt when Nick first asked the question of me!

I was fond of our times together. We would eat at several places—mostly at Maggiano's, Cheesecake Factory and a few times at Ferrari's Italian Restaurant in Madeira. Eventually these lunches became my own version of *Tuesdays with Morrie*. These one-on-one times with Nick through those years are special, cherished moments for me.

Then along the way, Joey Bianco joined us. Nick was a wonderful conduit for Joey to ease the pain of the difficulties he endured from his family. Joey and I both feel Nick's influence on us to this day. Once or twice a week, when he and I are on the phone talking over some life experience, we say to each other, "Remember what Nick would say: 'Guys, let it go!'"

There is no way that I can write out all the special moments of our lives spent with Nick! I hope it is sufficient to say that I loved Nick dearly! Nick was special because in a world that deals in chaos, he could embody our cultural upbringing and the values our parents instilled. Nick would say, "Through God's help, He will make the difference."

## Cheryl A. Marty, RN, BSN

To know Nick is to know humor, wisdom, and kindness, to be uplifted, to be heard, to be cherished, to be loved, and to be the recipient of donuts. I knew Nick as a manager of his primary physician's office. Nick was a giver in all ways possible. He loved a good donut and he liked to share his love of donuts with us. To think of him walking in with a smile and donuts just makes my heart melt. Beyond that, it was his kind heart that made every one of us feel important and cherished. He had a knack for making you feel cared about and he was truly interested in hearing what you had to say. He was a wealth of wisdom, and if you were listening, he would be teaching you a moral tidbit or lesson about life. Nick is dearly missed; however, his spirit is so full and alive in his memory that he will never be forgotten by those who knew him. I learned many life lessons from Nick and because of him, I am a better person and working hard to try and pay his spirit forward, along with a few donuts.

## Zina Siragusa

Nick Seta took an interest in everyone around him and the youth of our church were no exception. Captivated by his magic tricks, entertained by his humor, and blessed by his attitude and love, so many of our church's children were educated and equipped for God's kingdom without realizing it.

For my impressionable, eager-to-please young boy with boundless energy and a short attention span, God knew Nick was just what he needed. Nick took Jonathan under his wing like he did so many others. It was easy to see from the look in Jonathan's eyes that he saw Nick as a hero and a leader. Jonathan's rapid recount of Wednesday night church frequently included a long walk to McDonald's where Nick imparted wisdom along the way and filled a growing boy's belly too. Nick's lessons didn't require a classroom. They were imparted in a gritty real life way that my son, who'd prefer not to open a book, could live out. Jonathan grew in his understanding. His faith grew stronger week by week. He became a teenage boy who looked forward to church and seeing his mentor.

As Jonathan grew up, Nick's response to him changed to that of a man-to-man relationship. There was pride in Jonathan's expression as he was respected and valued by his hero. I truly think he felt more of a man because Nick believed in him.

Jonathan became a husband and a father and lived a short life that included a faith that did not waver. When I mourn the loss of my son in this life, I have to pause and be thankful for Nick, a faithful servant of God who helped to provide Jonathan with the directions home.

## Ken Nichols
(remarks delivered at Nick's memorial service in 2016)

What I would typically do for a memorial service I have chosen not to do, for this is a memorial service for someone who was anything but typical. For over 25 years I have been Nick's preacher. I have 25 years of experiences with Nick and a paltry few minutes to share them. Nick was a graduate and a teacher in a traditional Catholic School where Latin was taught. He and I shared a love for words. He used to say, "Words mean something. Choose your words wisely." He liked boiling things down to just a few words. So, I thought I would do that for us in this service.

### Words or phrases that remind me of Nick Seta:

*Irrepressible* – I remember being in Nick's company 20 years ago down at the Hamilton County Courthouse. I was shadowing Nick for the day at his invitation. We skipped every elevator or escalator that we encountered. "Take the stairs," Nick said. "It will keep you young."

When Nick was in his early 80's I can tell you that I would NOT want to have gone up against him in a street fight. . . .

I have to confess that even now what we are doing seems surreal. If ever there was someone who I knew with boundless energy and zeal for life, someone who could outlast them all, it was Nick Seta.

My children's' response to news of Nick's serious illness mirrored my own… "There must be some mistake….not Nick!?"

*Italian* – Nick was incurably Italian. He would remind me regularly that Rome was the mightiest civilization in human history. I would remind him that they never conquered Scotland.

Nick would remind me that Paul was a citizen of Rome. I would remind him that Paul considered himself the least of the Apostles.

***Politically incorrect*** – Only Nick could say the things that Nick could say. Only Nick could call the preacher's wife a "Sharp Broad" and no one would blink. Nick could tell anyone, "Do what you should do, you Little Puke" and they would take it as a compliment.

***Marine*** – Nick was rightfully proud of his service to our country in WW2. He did what hundreds of thousands of his fellow service men did on the beaches of the Japanese Islands and throughout Europe. He would tell you that he only did what a good Marine should do. I would tell you that he and his comrades saw and experienced things that no kid should be asked to experience and that what they did was nothing short of heroic. What Nick and others did, saved the world and made possible the American way of life that we routinely take for granted.

***Unambiguous*** – I never had to wonder what Nick thought. I always knew where I stood with him. A few times he read me the riot act. I listened because I knew he cared. Good, bad, or indifferent, he always spoke his mind . . . in language that could not be misunderstood.

***Inquisitive*** – Nick may have aged (eventually) but he was never too old to wonder, ask, or learn. Part of what made him an excellent teacher was that he was an excellent student. Many people in the context of the church (Bible class, et cetera) reach the point where they suppose that they have heard it all before. Nick continued to learn.

No one called me more often about a point of Scripture or theology than Nick. It often took place about breakfast time . . . I could tell that he was engaged in an argument over some point of the Bible with Lynn and he was calling to have me set her straight.

***Perceptive/Insightful*** – I expect I will never meet anyone who is able to read people like Nick Seta. He had a gift for looking at a person, their body language, the way they carry themselves, their interaction or lack thereof, and knowing that something was not right. Dozens of times he would alert me to see what is going on in the life of a church member because he could tell something was not right. He was almost always right!

***Logical*** – Nick spoke hundreds of times all around the country. As a keynote speaker, he was known especially among the military, educators and police. I was blessed to go several times and share in Nick's addresses. He used one of the rarest and most powerful of subjects: *common sense*. He told me more than once that he had made a good living telling people what they should have already known, but they were just too smart for their own good.

***Self aware*** – Nick was not just a good reader of people; he knew himself very well also. He was not perfect, and never had any notions that such was the case. As a result, he was grounded and aware of his own shortcomings. As a result, he knew his own need for forgiveness and found it easier to seek the help of God along the way.

***Encourager*** – Nick took the pragmatic application of the teaching of Jesus to heart. As such he made it his mission to encourage everyone he came into contact with. A waitress in a restaurant, a homeless man on a downtown street, a kid in the church lobby . . . Nick left everyone with the impression that they were important and that they mattered.

***Friend*** – If there were ever a serious fight, I would want Nick Seta on my side. Nick and my Dad were born (about) the same year. My Dad passed away 18 years before him. Since that time, I have shared scores of lunches and hundreds of hours of talk with Nick. For that I will be forever grateful.

***Disciple*** – Nick was a student of the teaching of Jesus Christ, a disciple in the truest sense of the word. And I do not mean by that, that Nick was merely an intellectual who dabbled in the teachings of Christ the Teacher. Nick was sinner, saved by God's grace, who trusted in Jesus Christ and hoped in Him.

# Transcript of Columbus Day Dinner Speech for The Sons of Italy

Greetings, Judge Panioto informed me that approximately one-half of this audience was Italian and that the other half was desperately trying to become Italian.

We're here this evening to commemorate the accomplishments of Christopher Columbus. I was born in Southern Italy in an area called Calabria. That makes me Calabrese. The town I was born in, high up in the mountains, is called Fuscaldo. That makes me Fuscaldese. As a youngster in school, I never let anyone forget that Christopher Columbus, an Italian, had discovered our hemisphere. I never let anyone forget that America was named after America Vespucci, another Italian. I took great pride in Michael Angelo, DaVinci, and others. But that for which I am the most thankful to my Italian heritage is the love it instilled in me for family, for children, for God, and the respect it ingrained in me for positions of authority.

When taking on the privilege of speaking to an audience, I always try to have the integrity to limit myself to that which I have established some credibility based on commitment, performance and experience. I have only two such areas; one is the area of gambling. As many of you in this audience know, I am somewhat gifted with cards and have spent some time in the world of professional gambling. The other area is young people; specifically their problems, their behavior. My entire public career has been in working with the children of this community.

Since I'm not going to do a gambling show, I want to address you with a great deal of concern about our young people and their problems.

The majority of kids are in good shape, however, there are far too many youngsters who are having far too many problems that are far too serious in relationship to the opportunities they have in life in this nation.

It is unacceptable to me that in the area of violent crime, the darkest cloud hanging over our nation, a cloud that has literally lowered our quality of life (rape, murder, assault, et cetera), close to fifty percent of this crime is committed by an age group that spans six years, ages fourteen to nineteen years. That is unacceptable. In the area of drugs, their participation is massive and continuing to increase, which is unacceptable. In the area of alcohol, their participation is massive and continuing to grow, which is unacceptable. In the area of suicide, their participation is pandemic, not epidemic, that is unacceptable.

When we hear these things, we always ask, "Why?" Why is this happening? We all know there is no single cause-and-effect answer to a phenomenon as complex as human behavior. However, let me assure you there is a flaw that's been growing in this country. Much like the flaw in a woman's nylon, it starts ever so small and then spreads through the entire stocking. That is the flaw called the "Lack of Personal Discipline." Let's immediately distinguish between control and personal discipline. Control is the external application of force for the modification of behavior. That's not what personal discipline is. Personal discipline is that voice inside of us that is supposed to boom at us, "No, I will not do that because it offends my community, family, God, but most importantly, it offends me" Ladies and Gentlemen, not only is that voice not booming, it's not even a whisper. The reason it is not booming is that the voice is an ability. And like all abilities, it must be taught, learned and practiced. Parents must teach it, children must learn it, and both must practice it. And in the same way you develop basketball skills by practicing with a ball and a basket, you develop the skills of personal discipline by practicing with the sacred cows of your society—the sacred cows of clergy, teachers, parents, police, et cetera.

I want all of you in this room to do something for me. Go back in your memory and place yourself as a young kid in your living room, seated beside your father. A member of the clergy walks in, and you say, "Hi, Rev." What would have happened to you? I would have been bounced off the wall, and so would many of you. We were taught to limit our behavior and restrict our tongue. We were taught to respect the position of authority. That is no longer the case. Too many parents of the last generation have thought it fashionable to castigate authority in front of and with their kids. Many is the time, I've heard parents say to their children, "They should stop teachers from giving homework," or "Is your counselor stupid? Look at this schedule," or "Another tax levy, all they do is ask for money and improve nothing." Now I'm not saying there are not teachers, counselors or boards that need to be scrutinized. What I'm saying is we should do it in private as adults. If there is anything that kids do not need our help in doing, it is in tearing down the positions of authority. They are born with that talent. They must be taught to respect the position of authority regardless of the person in it.

I was baptized Catholic. In southern Italy, you are baptized Catholic, or they throw you into the Mediterranean Sea. It's called an offer you can't refuse. I know there were a couple of popes who had children. Popes are not supposed to have babies. Does that give me the right to challenge the papacy? No. It merely means there were a couple of popes who zigged when they should have zagged. However, let's keep history straight. Those were French and Spanish popes before the Italian popes took over.

What happened? What caused us to go astray? Keep in mind it didn't happen overnight. It takes time for cultural change to come to fruition. There are three factors that have and continue to contribute to the problems. The first is the philosophy of permissiveness, whose basic tenet is you must not use punishment for the correction of behavior. Punishment causes hostility and is abusive. And by implication, anyone who uses it is an abuser. The advocates of this philosophy infiltrated our academic world at all levels and strongly influenced the fields of education, psychology and journalism. They violated the most fundamental principle of human nature: that the only thing that alters human behavior positively or negatively is consequence. In the place of consequence, they substituted insight. Their dogma believes that if you allow a child to view and understand the destructiveness of his behavior, he will be motivated to change. So if a child pulls down a lamp, a picture, or an antique, you do not spank, you do not smack his hand, instead, you make him step back and view the destructiveness of his behavior, and he will be self-motivated to change. Folks, that is not only intellectual insanity, it is tragically self-destructive. And these individuals have had a tremendous impact on our present-day attitudes toward punishment. It is not fashionable or safe to admit you spank your child. Mothers are afraid to spank a child in a supermarket, or a department store, who is touching and messing with items, violating store rules. Mothers are afraid to spank their children for fear of being reported, charged or arrested. A 911-call causes the mandatory arrest of the person charged. Kids know this. Being what they are, they manipulate it into a power base. They threaten parents; they threaten teachers. Teachers are afraid to touch a kid, fearful of what the child might do with that touch. We have castrated parents and teachers in their ability to deal with their children. They have become tentative, cautious, fearful and angry. We have given children more rights to destroy themselves than we have rights to protect them. The tail is now wagging the dog. All one has to do is look at our schools, our streets, our cities.

    The second factor was the Spock phenomenon. It has had a great impact on us. I am not here to criticize Dr. Spock. He was sincere. But without intending to do so, and I say this because thirty-some years later, much too late, he wrote his second book in which he apologized for what he had written and admitted his errors. But what he did was resurrect the doctrine of determinism. He attempted to respond to the parents of his time. These parents had watched industry, business, and education send their supervisors and teachers to seminars and workshops and get books and tapes to learn how to handle employees and students. They wanted the same help to handle children. So Dr. Spock wrote his book. Unfortunately, he wrote it like a science book, using scientific methods with empirical conclusions. A+B=C. And that's exactly how he wrote his book. He told parents you do ABC & D correctly, and your kids will do EFG & H. America believed him. Parents did ABC & D, but the kids did not do EFG & H. It was at this precise moment that the seeds were sown for one of our worst problems. Parents began to embrace the blame and responsibility for their children's behavior. They had been told if they did things right, the kids would turn out right. Since they didn't turn out right, it had to be them. So they began to ask, "Where did we go wrong?" "What didn't we do that we should have done?" It wasn't the kid's fault; it was theirs. And the social engineers reinforced it all with their chant that "Yes, it was the environment and those bad mommas and poppas." Out of this, slowly but surely, has grown the dogma we have today, that everybody is a victim of society. People commit murder, rape, abuse, whatever, and the first thing we do is look for the "root cause" that explains it all. Personal responsibility and accountability have gone out the window.

The third and most important factor has been the abdication of the male. We convinced ourselves our kids had to have "everything we didn't have" and "nothing was going to be too good for our kids." We got caught up in a whirlpool of affluence, working late, meetings, out-of-town conferences, the whole nine yards, but in the meantime, we abdicated our role in the decision-making level of our families. I speak to many groups of school administrators. If I would ask an audience of school principals, "If a kid gets in trouble in school, who calls the school, dad or mom?" The loud response is Mom. If someone had to come to the school, would it be dad or mom? The loud response is Mom. At the juvenile court, if we don't subpoena Dad; it's

Mom. You cannot have that kind of imbalance. God and nature tell us to maintain balance or we will suffer distortion. Ladies and gentlemen, regardless of what any group or movement wants to proclaim, there is a difference between motherhood and fatherhood. God put together Adam and Eve, not Adam and Steve. Motherhood in nature is protective of its flock. I don't care if it's a mamma human, or a mamma tiger, lion, baboon, or bear; don't mess with their young. Motherhood protects and nurtures. Fatherhood, on the other hand, is warrior, provider, and hunter. Power and authority is his game. He identifies with the position of authority and the people in it. That is why, ladies and gentlemen, if we got in trouble in school, we were automatically in trouble at home. If we got a tail-kicking in school, we got one at home. If we got in trouble with a neighbor, a police officer, a clergyman, the formula was the same. Our fathers did not ask how did it happen. They supported the positions of authority. My father never asked me did I have a good time in school, did I like my teacher? He had two questions for me every night: "E statto boune ogge?" "Et che ta barrota ogge?" I wasn't the greatest of students, so I gave him Columbus on Monday, Washington on Tuesday and Lincoln on Wednesday. Strong, involved fatherhood neutralizes permissiveness and imposes personal accountability and responsibility. Fatherhood needs to step forward. Unfortunately, close to fifty percent of American kids are being raised in homes without fathers.

 In my closing remarks, I want to draw our attention to two forces that are ripping the fiber of this nation. The first is the open attack on the positions of authority and the people in it. It has become open season for rip, tear and destroy. The American public has been convinced and conditioned that we cannot trust senators, representatives, presidents, judges, police officers, bosses, or anyone in authority. I ask these people, with what do you replace authority? How does a collective society survive without positions of authority? And, of course, young people feed off of this garbage. They love the mentality that says, "Do your own thing; grab your own bag. If it feels good, do it." And they've been terribly successful. One of the saddest things I can say to you tonight is that, at this moment in time, it is impossible for us to have a hero in our nation. As soon as we put anyone up, they immediately start tearing him down. And if they have to go back twenty five years to where this guy peed behind the school, they'll dig up the cement to prove it.

The second is this obsession we have with the rights of the individual. I know we live in a collective society that must hang in a tender balance. But they must always tilt in favor of the collective society. The individual cannot be greater than his society. That is the quickest and surest path to self-destruction.

This is the "Columbus Day Italian Dinner" and many of our relatives as well as we ourselves are proud to be Italians and blessed to be Americans. Let us be aware and be involved and be the people who make a difference in the lives of our family, community and in our nation. Remember these two quotes. "The only thing necessary for the triumph of evil is for good men to do nothing." "The voices of the few are greatly magnified by the silence of the many." Let us not do nothing. Let us not be silent.

# Photos from Nick's History

Mountain town of Fuscaldo, Italy, castle ruins on top right

Panorama of Fuscaldo

Walls of convent in Fuscaldo

From a church porch, the next street up

St. Joseph Church, Fuscaldo

Stone steps found in the interior of Fuscaldo and a door to a home. There are many cats in Fuscaldo.

Bed Nick was born in, Fuscaldo

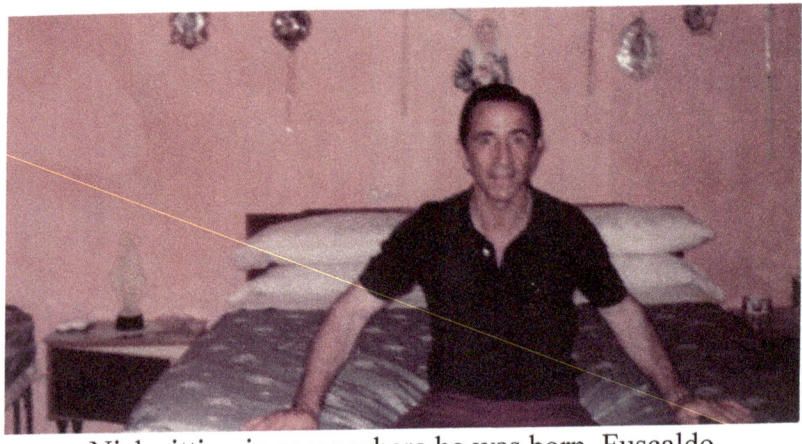
Nick sitting in room where he was born, Fuscaldo

Francesco and Maria Seta

Melina Seta, June, 1925 Nick's sister

Nick as baby in Fuscaldo

Manifest of President Wilson sailed from Napoli October 14, 1927

Nick with mom and dad, 1927 in Cincinnati

Nick             Nick and Dad

St. Mary's School, 2nd grade

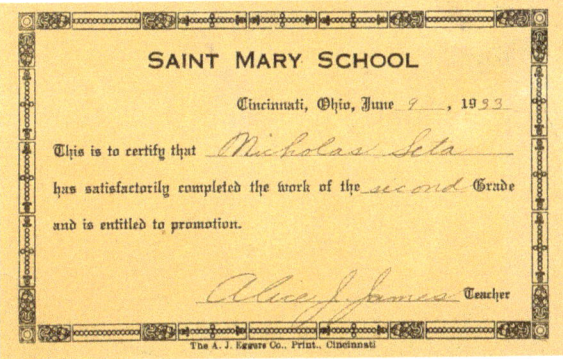

St. Mary's School Promotion Card, June 9, 1933

St. Mary's Class, Nick sitting 2nd from right

St. Mary's Diploma from 8th Grade

Nick with parents, Age 12

Graduation from Purcell High School, June 1943, Age 17

Marines, 1944, Age 18

Nick with Marine buddy having fun

Nick with Mom and Dad in the late 1940s

Children's Unit School, Longview State Hospital, 1950, old TB ward

Front door of Children's Unit School

Bell donated to Children's Unit school by
William S. Murell Co. May 4, 1961

Swimming Pool at Longview State Hospital

Porch of Children's Unit School – Nick with donors to school

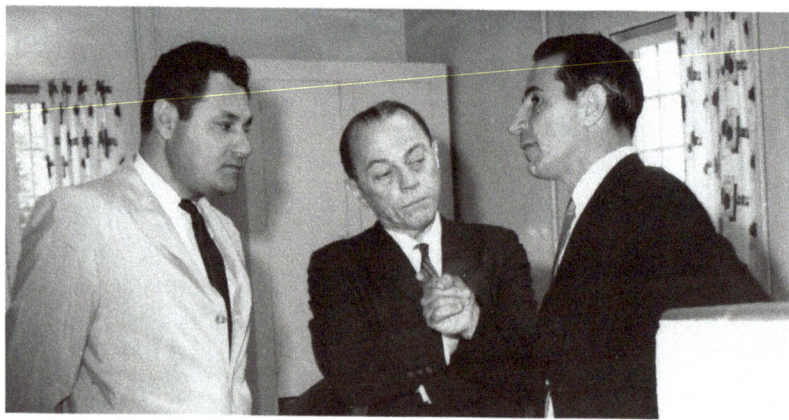
Judge Benjamin Schwartz and Dr. Baltazar Anaya in CUS Home Economics Room

Mr. Harris, Director of Personnel at LSH, Dr. Kahlily, Psychiatrist at the CUS, Mr. Lanier, Business Director of LSH, and Nick

Dr. Marty Kishner and Dr. Kahlily, Psychiatrists of CUS

Nick in classroom at the CUS

Cousins to Nick, brothers Joe and John Seta

Cousins Carlo, John and Don Seta with Nick

Cousins Carol, Don and friend Tony with Nick

Nick with Cousins, Don, Seated Carlo, Uncle Joe and Bill

Nick with Judge Ben Schwartz, Hamilton County Juvenile Court with Chick Chelekis, Probation Officer, Unknown Lady

Nick with dear friend Chick Chelekis

# Nick in the News

## Problems of youth topic of Kiwanis Club speaker

Nick A. Seta, director of the Children's Unit at Longview State Hospital gave the Norwood Kiwanis Club some hard hitting pointers on what to do about the young last Thursday at Quality Courts Motel.

He explained why children even in the lower grades don't identify with the problems of their community and nation and don't have the set of values that their parents and grandparents had.

They are taught values in the home, school and church but as soon as they hit the street they are taken over by the underground which tells them that honesty and other things their parents took for granted don't count. They are taught that all that counts are material things, how big a car do you have, how many cigarets can you smoke, and how much can you drink. Have you tried marijuana—the older folks themselves can't agree whether it is bad or not so why not try it. They are taught "To hell with what went on before."

Seta sees the solution as return to the town meeting, to making religion and morals relevant in the pulpit, and to do away with the permissiveness that covers American life. He castigated lawyers who make it almost impossible to get a conviction of children or adults who violate the law and put off indefinitely or forever conviction of those who have the money to pay for it even if they sold drugs to get it.

Norwood Enterprise
Nov. 5, 1970.

## Nick Seta to Speak at Indian Hill Junior High

INDIAN HILL — One of Cincinnati's most dynamic speakers, Nick Seta, will address the parents of the Indian Hill Junior High School students, on Thursday, November 5, at 8 p.m. in the school's cafeteria. Mr. Seta, Director of the Children's Unit School at Longview State Hospital, will speak on parental responsibility and drug abuse. Uniquely enough, Mr. Seta is also known as Professor of psychology at Xavier University; retired professional gambler; active professional showman; selftaught genius with a deck of cards; advanced amateur philosopher; knowledgeable student of history; athlete; connoisseur of probabilities; able handler of dice.

Sponsored by the Mental Health Committee of the Indian Hill Junior-Senior High School PTA, this program will

# Seta 'Really Tells It Like He Sees It;' Cites Need for Volunteers At Longview

### BY PEGGY GRIFFIN

"Man, he really tells it like he sees it." This comment was typical of those heard after the March 13 FAST, featuring Nick Seta, Chairman of the Department of Education at Longview State Hospital. Mr. Seta addressed the audience on "Children of Longview."

Mr. Seta

"Eight years ago," Mr. Seta began, "we had 35 kids at Longview. An official count today shows that there are 267 kids at Longview. There has got to be something wrong in a country as great as ours when this many kids are ending up in mental hospitals."

Seta felt that our permissive society has been a great factor in the increased number of young mental patients. "I consider myself a disciplinarian and an authoritarian. This doesn't mean that I get down on the kids all the time; it means that I'm trying to say to them, 'I love ya so much that I don't want ya to do the wrong thing.'"

"Parents don't realize that children are begging sometimes, 'Please say no to me,'" he said. "I'm not against turning kids loose; I'm against turning them loose too soon, when there is a greater chance of their getting confused and picking up distortions."

"You know," Seta continued, "raising money for Longview is the easiest job I have there. I'm not saying raising money is easy, but it's a hell of a lot easier than getting human involvement. I just can't get human involvement, activism, participation — whatever you want to call it. All I get is talk."

Commenting on this lack of involvement, Seta said, "American youth are the greatest youth in the world. Sure, they're wrapped up in dissent, but dissent can be one way of progress. Notice I sad *one* way. The trouble is, all I get is dissent and talk.

Everybody wants to play the talking game, but nobody wants to play the playing game."

Mr. Seta explained that one of his functions at Longview is to recruit youth to work in their spare time with the in-patient children.

"There are so many of you guys who sit in the dorms on Sunday afternoons hashing over a lot of pseudo-intellectual horsecrap. You talk about helping people, but to help people you must get together with people. Let's get off this pseudo stuff. If you want to help people, get off your fanny and help. I'm talking about helping the most deprived kinds in the world. The damnable disability of not being able to use your mind — I get the idea that this is the toughest there is."

"You know, out of this entire student body, Chip Carpenter (XU Junior) and about seven other guys come to take out 30 kids once or twice a week. How many of you can't give an hour and a half of your time a week to help some kid?"

Mr. Seta explained that he is not necessarily looking for student volunteers who are psychology or sociology majors. "All it takes to get along with people is a little body chemistry. In fact, in my humble, egotistical opinion, I think you (psychiatrists and sociologists) stink. All you do is research and talk to me about some kid's basic hangup, but you won't tell me how to work with it. I want to know what I can do about a particular kid's acne, about making sure there's food in his stomach, about getting him a membership to the WMCA. I'm so sick and tired of research, especially on white rats. I've never met a white rat yet that could read."

After the talk, Chip Carpenter announced that there would be a big drive to recruit students to join the Student Volunteer Services.

"If anyone is interested in helping now," Chip stated, he or she can contact me or contact the Student Volunteer Services. This organization's pet project at the present time is doing recreational work with youngsters at Longview State Mental Hospital; they also have approximately eleven other programs in which they participate, such as the Big Brother program and work in the Appalachia area."

Xavier University March 15, 1970

# conversation

## It's Not Easy To Give Child What He Needs

**BY GEORGE PALMER**
Enquirer Reporter

Nick Seta is sort of a firecracker who talks in a series of explosions. A portrait in print reads: "... was a dealer at 14 in Northern Kentucky clubs... a Marine at 17... action in the South Pacific... came back ... dealer in Reno, Vegas... no longer a professional gambler... put on gambling shows to demonstrate cheating... born in Fuscaldo in southern Italy... went to Xavier University on GI Bill... took a degree in history, later a masters in education... now teach sike of delink (psychology of delinquency) at XU, also guiding the emotionally disturbed child..." Nicholas Andrew Seta is associate professor of psychology at XU and "general handyman" at Longview State Hospital where he is principal of the children's unit. On January 9 Seta takes on still another activity when he begins teaching a course on behavioral disorders of children at Northern Kentucky University.

Question: What will be the thrust of the new course?

Seta: What I'm going to try to produce in the class is a sense of enthusiasm that we should have for children. Teachers, social workers, educators, psychiatrists, psychologists, parents—all are seeking an easy way to handle human behavior. There is no such thing. I'll try to create in people (in the class) the anticipation that kids are hell on wheels. They are not changed very easily; there is no panacea, no aspirin. No parent-teacher conference can change it. It's a matter of getting in there and taking a beating and saying I love it and, baby, I'm going to handle it. When you project that, the kids will love you for it.

Question: How do you project that image to children?

Seta: Discipline is the key to human behavior. That doesn't mean rigidity or punishment. It just means once you say you are going to do something, and you have the ability to do it, you have a commitment to get it done. Kids need that kind of role model. If there's anyone I can't stand—and kids can't stand—it's the undisciplined disciplinarian. I mean the guy who says you're going to do this, you're going to do that. His very example is the opposite of what he's saying to kids. This turns them off.

Kids do respect power and authority because they understand that figure of authority can give structure to their lives, help them achieve their goals and bring them into line. Kids need that. Kids hold on to that individual who shows he has power and authority but uses it in a sense of affection toward the child, in a sense of limit-setting, always letting the kid know he is sitting on the kid's behavior.

Question: Are parents, teachers and other educators forwarding that image?

Seta: I don't think many of us working with kids really understand the sense of responsibility we have—that in our hands we have minds we can actually affect. We have to make an imprint on children. I remember my grade school and high school and college teachers because they made an imprint on me that has never left. I don't think kids of today are getting that kind of imprint. We're overloading classes and using departmentalized education in the early grades. Kids see six and seven teachers a day. Actually, the way a kid learns best is to identify with a single adult. He wants to be like you so he begins to do it for you and not just for himself. You're leading him, not pushing him.

Question: What other factors might lead to behavorial disorders in children?

Seta: For one, the disappearance of the extended family in America. What we have today are little microfamilies—husband, wife and child. That's no family... it's three human beings trying to make it, very little giving, very little sharing. If there's anything the human being does not need, it's an exercise in selfishness. We need an exercise in giving. You know, once upon a time kids heard the same things at home, school and church—three rings that were joined. Today those rings are adversaries. The family is over here, school is out there and the church is trying to find out

Enquirer photo BY TOM HUBBARD

## HISTORY OF THE FUSCALDESE —

In the early years of the 20th century a small group of Fuscaldesi settled in Cincinnati. However, it was not until the end of World War I that they arrived in appreciable numbers. They were attracted to the Queen City by the promise of immediate employment. Cincinnati was virgin territory for their field of specialty — technical tailors. Since that time they have assumed the leading role in the tailoring field and hold many of the responsible positions in this industry.

A steady migration of Fuscaldesi continued until 1924, when the Immigration Law of that year, known as the Johnson Act, drastically curtailed the entrance of Europeans to our nation.

These immigrants faced the eternal problem of all migratory people, that of adjustment to a new environment. Language, customs, traditions all presented distinct problems to the solution of adequate socialization in the New World.

From their love of music a fine band was born. It was directed by the late Professor Raffaele Seta and was affiliated with the Italian War Veterans of Cincinnati. But this activity, fine though it be, was too limited and could not provide sufficient activities to meet the general needs of the total population. They needed an organization that would provide social gatherings. That would provide a place and occasion for them to express their views, attitudes and concepts in their native tongue, until such time that mastery of the new language was acquired.

So it was that in Feb. of 1930 a small band of Fuscaldesi, realizing the dire need that existed, organized the Fuscaldese Society. This organization provided the atmosphere needed for the solution of problems related to this transitional period. Down through the years it has extended sick benefits and other forms of aid to its members in need.

The vast majority of present-day Fuscaldesi are American citizens, serving America with the pride and passion so characteristic of a Latin people. In World War II practically all their available young men served in the U.S. Armed Forces.

The modern generation of Fuscaldesi, not burdened with the barriers faced by their forefathers, have achieved the fine accomplishments of higher education. As a result you will find them dotted throughout the many professional areas enjoying the success of a people determined to succeed.

These young people represent the contribution to our American heritage and their sole aim shall always be, **A GREATER AMERICA UNDER GOD!**

Nicholas A. Seta<br>President

AUTO — FIRE — LIABILITY — INSURANCE
RELIABLE INSURING AGENCY
Frank Novelli - Representative
2421 Highland Ave.  AV 1-8709

History of Fuscaldese written by Nick Seta

# AN EVENING WITH NICK SETA

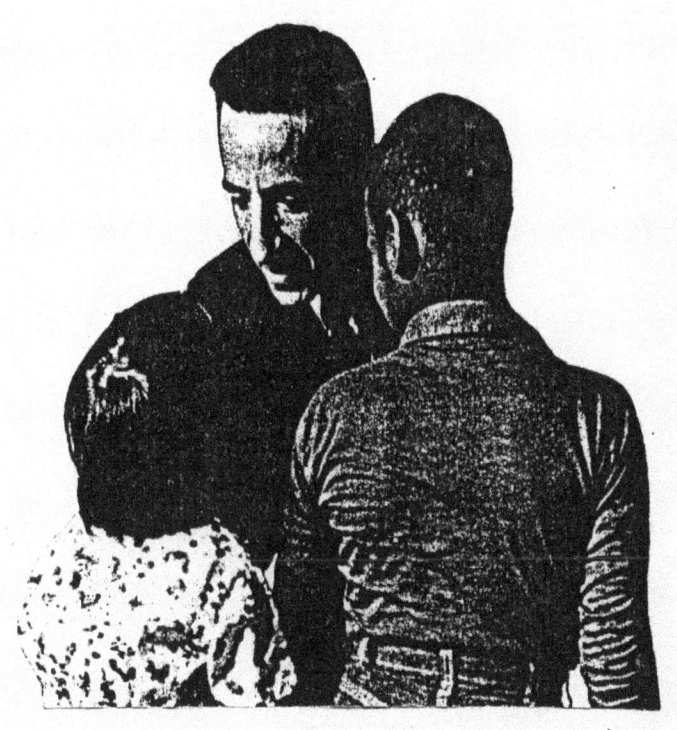

Co-Sponsored by the:

Council for Exceptional Children, Tuscho Chapter 840, and East Central Ohio Special Education Regional Resource Center

## TOPIC

"10 Commandments In Handling Surface Behavior"

## DATE
April 26, 1982

## TIME
6:00 P.M.

## LOCATION
Zoar Hotel
Zoar, Ohio

## Nick Seta

Nicholas Andrew Seta, the only son of an immigrant barber, was born in the southern Italian seacoast town of Fuscaldo. At the age of three he emigrated to the United States with his family. He grew up during the Depression and shares with his contemporaries the singular pride of having lived to tell about it.

Nick Seta earned BA and MEd degrees from Xavier University. He is well known as the founder and administrator of the Children's Unit School at Longview State Hospital from 1950 to 1980.

Nick also initiated the educational program at the Hamilton County Juvenile Center in Cincinnati and is now that court's administrator.

He is associate professor at Xavier University in the area of emotional disturbance and lectures throughout the country on family and juvenile discipline and surface behavior.

Nick has won the "Citizen of the Year Award" from the Ohio Child Conservation League, the "Exceptional Service" award from Hamilton County Division of Police, and "Outstanding Achievement" awards from the Cincinnati Division of Police and the President's Commission for the Handicapped.

Nick is known to many as a professor, retired gambler, professional showman, philosopher, student of history, and an athlete. Most importantly, he cares and is concerned about children.

## 10 COMMANDMENTS
## IN HANDLING SURFACE BEHAVIOR

1. SOMETIMES IT'S BETTER NOT TO SEE OR HEAR . . .

    Planned ignoring is the intuitive ability to select which behavior to intervene with and which to ignore . . . One cannot interfere with all of his groups irritating behavior and be effective . . . This technique permits the draining and dissipation of tensions and allows the youngster to stop his own behavior . . . (tattling, mumbling, snooping, etc.)

    NOTES:

2. USE A SIGN, SOUND OR LOOK . . .

    In many instances, a work or motion can provide enough intervening support to enable a youngster to handle his impulses. Such actions as yelling, cursing, jumping, etc., can often be stopped by a simple sign, sound or look . . . So often we raise the roof when we need only to raise our eyebrows.

    NOTES:

3. <u>GET'EM OVER THE HUMP</u> . . .
This is the well timed boost given to a kid that helps him over a hump blocking his way to a goal . . . This will often spell the difference between a rage outburst and success . . . If the hurdle help is given at the right moment, the youngster is usually able to go on and his undesirable behavior is <u>prevented</u> . . .

NOTES:

4. <u>BECOME ONE OF THEIR FANS</u> . . .
Their lives have been filled with failures . . . They've not succeeded too often or do they believe they can . . . Build them up by showing interest in their work, projects, play, etc. . . . Exude praise and amazement over their accomplishments . . . Show excitement with them about their successes . . . They love phrases such as, "Did you do that by yourself?", "Is this really yours?" "When did you get that good?"

NOTES:

5. THROW THAT "CHANGE-UP" . . .
A major league pitcher always has a change-up to throw when his regular stuff is going sour . . . A teacher must have this same ability. He must be sensitive to switching from an activity that is temporarily going sour, to one more desirable. Sometimes a brand new activity is needed, other times just a break. Youngsters will act-out when the situation they are in is ineffective . . . The timing of these switches must be a "planned control" technique.

NOTES:

6. BE SPECIFIC, CONSISTENT AND SIMPLE IN YOUR RULES . . . (SIMPLE, DIRECT AND CORRECT)
This is especially true with young children. Tell them what you want and how it is to be done. Keep procedures simple, complexity lends itself to confusion and disobedience. Once your requests are known, maintain consistency . . . An organized house routine not only tells kids what is expected of them, but what they can expect in return. ISN'T THIS WHAT WE ALL WANT IN OUR JOBS?

NOTES:

7. **USE THE POSITIVE RATHER THAN THE NEGATIVE** . . .

   Too often we violate this rule by ignoring youngsters until they misbehave, thus focusing their attention on incorrect behavior . . . Too often we use negative statements of control. We'll say "Take your feet off the chair", when we should say "Put your feet on the floor". Or we say "Stop leaving your coats on the chairs", instead of "Hang up your coat". Negative statements <u>do not tell</u> a youngster what to do.

NOTES:

8. **SAVE YOUR THREATS** . . .

   You usually regret making them anyway . . . However, once made, you better carry them out. If you don't, youngsters learn to disregard them causing more acting-out . . . Too often we can't even carry out our threats.

NOTES:

9. TRUST 'EM . . .

When a youngster gives you an excuse or reason explaining his behavior, (Is late, library, etc.) accept it. CHECK LATER . . . In this way the kid has no out of "not being trusted". "Everybody questions me", etc.

NOTES:

10. BE JUST . . .

If you do not witness an accident, handle all parties alike, ignore or give equal treatment. (BEWARE OF YOUR BIASES; SELF-FULFILLING PROPHECIES.)

NOTES:

"HE TOUCHES LIVES"
Reprinted from the
Cincinnati Enquirer, Sunday Magazine
February 29, 1976

Had Nick Seta been peddling stocks, insurance, used cars or vacuum cleaners for the past 25 years, he probably would be filthy rich and you probably would own at least one of whatever he had been selling.

Instead, the only son of an Italian immigrant barber "got hooked" in 1950 on the emotionally disturbed kids at Longview State Hospital.

In the dozen or so speaking engagements he has each month, the skillfully aggressive Nick Seta uses his many talents as a salesman, former gambler, wizard with a deck of cards, astute student of history and philosophy, former juvenile court officer and entertaining and provocative lecturer to gain public support for the children's school he directs.

His pitch has been so successful that community groups such as Kiwanis Clubs, Jaycees, television personalities like Ruth Lyons and Bob Braun, area department stores and many others have responded by donating as much as $20,000 annually to "Nick's kids."

This steady flow of contributions has meant a pool table, tape recorders, typewriters, money for special parties and treats, recreation equipment, school supplies, a summer camp program and about 30 "visiting friends" or volunteers to the 80 children in the school unit.

To Nick Seta, who prefers to credit community support rather than his own instinctive hustling for making this possible, it has meant Longview's program has survived and prospered. While similar ones at other state mental institutions have struggled and sometimes gone under due to the "ebbs and tides" of state funding, Longview's has received local, state and some national recognition and publicity.

If Nick Seta has been so successful, why hasn't he been lured away by some slick public relations firm?

"Don't think they haven't tried!" replies Seta with mock modesty. "There are a number of fields I could have cleaned up in , but so far I haven't had an offer that compares to this."

"After I fell into this job, with some encouragement, I realized how much opportunity there was to do things for these kids.

"In a regular school, teachers only care for a portion of the kid's needs. I'm involved with the kids' every emotional, psychological, physical, social and educational need 24 hours a day.

"It's an ego trip for me to have to try to meet all these needs," he says. "It's kind of like telling a narcissistic broad who loves clothes that she's got an unlimited budget."

"The needs are so great you can go in all directions. If you like it, is there anything better than doing what fulfills you emotionally and psychologically? It's a constant ball to me. I'm glad I'm making decent money , but it's the kind of thing I'd do for nothing."

"As long as you're hustling, Baby, someplace, somehow, somewhere you're helping somebody. You're touching the life of a kid. That's the beauty. Compare that to a job where you don't touch anybody."

It's hard to imagine Nick Seta not touching somebody. His hand is always out, his arm is usually around the person closest to him, his small, seemingly black eyes dart from person to person, leaving no one out, and his mouth, well, it never closes.

Try following the lithe Italian, born in the southern seacoast town of Fuscaldo but raised on the Cincinnati riverfront and the streets of Over-the-Rhine. He is 50, looks 30 and acts (sometimes) 16. He will run you ragged. His energy, his personality can't be contained. Those within reach can't ignore his opinions, and can't forget them weeks after the encounter.

When Nick Seta bounds out of his car at about 8 a.m. each weekday, he does not stop for the next 12 to 14 hours. After briefly checking in with his office staff, he heads for the daily accountability session with his 14 teachers and eight recreation workers.

Sitting atop a table in what is loosely referred to as the teachers' lounge, Seta fires questions at his staff: How are the plans for the party going? Do we have enough vans to take the kids to the theater? How's the newly admitted girl doing? Is the banjo act sure for the party?

The banjo player can't make it because he has to work, explains a teacher. "Call his boss," orders Seta. "If he understands what his employee is doing, he'll let him off. It is good public relations for him to be able to say one of his employees plays the banjo for the kids at Longview."

Greeting the children as they cover the 100 yards between the four residential units and the classroom building obviously is the high point of Seta's morning. Some children stroll the short distance; others run straight into the arms of Nick Seta.

"Hey, Mr. Dago," shouts one child, as Seta pats him on the rear. "At least they respect me," confides Seta. "They call me mister."

"What's the matter with you?" Seta quizzes another boy. "You don't look so good today." He shakes hands with some; smacks others on the cheeks. He teases the girls about their clothes and hairdos. "Here comes Miss America," he chides one girl.

Seta's goal is to get the children to respond, to react. He scoffs at child psychiatrists who would "get down on my rough-housing," saying it is necessary because "the world's not an easy place to grow up in, Baby."

Few school principals make general announcements to each class personally, but Seta has a habit of popping in and out of classrooms all day. This day he tells the children they will be getting two new outfits of clothes. One is theirs but the other must be kept at the school.

"Why can't we keep them both?" asks one girl. "Now, Judy, some of the kids who come here are not from good homes like yours. They don't have nice clothes like you do," Seta answers.

Seta joins a class in the library reading a story about a snake. "What kind of snake is it?" asks Seta. "A Dago snake," shouts one boy.

A girl is in tears in the home economics room, claiming several other girls hit her in her room this morning. Seta puts his arm around her, takes her aside and counsels her. Later, she runs up to him in the hall, hugs him and tells him she's sorry for "acting like a baby."

In shop class, Seta singles out one boy making wooden reindeer and the two serenade the class with "From one beer lover to another!"

"That kid," muses Seta. "I couldn't reach him until I heard him humming along with that television beer commercial." Now they have something to share.

Seta's ability to reach each child, no matter how severe his or her mental problems, hinges on establishing a unique, personal relationship with the child. To some children he's "father, mother, brother, you name it. Oh yeah, the girls sometimes get crushes on me, but what the hell. I'm a good looking Dago. Can you blame them?"

"Sure, some hate me, some love me, but they all know me."

Listening is an essential daily part of Seta's relationship with the psychiatric aides who staff the children's living units. "These people are good people, they have to be. Nobody else wants to work these wards. The kids are rough," he explains.

He sympathizes with their complaints about being understaffed—a common problem throughout Longview. "We've got one psych aide for 20 kids. If there were two people, we could do a decent job. As it is, we try harder, right?" he asks, nudging one worker into agreement.

After Seta has greeted every child and staff member, listened to every complaint and answered each question, he returns to his office to answer a backlog of telephone calls, talk with staff members and children individually, and shuffle papers.

His day is marked by one interruption after another, yet he rarely loses his train of thought, even after a lengthy phone call or a talk with a staff member about a problem.

By the time school is over in mid-afternoon, Seta is ready to join the children in a game of touch football or basketball. He doesn't hesitate pitting himself against a 6-foot, 180-pound adolescent boy despite his own lean 5-foot-6, 140-pound frame.

When he's not taking somebody on in a game of pool or dancing with the girls at the evening recreation sessions, he may be out doing a few card tricks for a men's club, women's club, country club, or church group and intermingling the needs of the kids at Longview.

A self-taught genius with a deck of cards, Seta was already dealing cards in Newport's gambling casinos as a teenager. His expertise with a deck of cards continued to win him cash during his stint in the Marines during World War II. After the war, he frequented West Coast gambling establishments and gradually drifted into the professional's world. His conscience eventually convinced him to change professions and he opted for a college education at Xavier University in the late 1940s.

"People wouldn't invite me just to talk about Longview," he admits casually. "It's that evil side of me--my years as a professional gambler--that gets me in."

"Man is more attracted to bad than good and don't let anybody tell you different. But if you can turn people on for whatever reason, you can get them interested in your cause."

What turns people on, according to Seta, are the "two Cs." If you've got chemistry and charisma, you can get people to do anything for you.

Whatever Nick Seta's got, people love it and it's helped get Longview a few things that he and the community can point to with pride.

The children's school unit, which began in a small building that formerly housed tuberculosis patients, now is a multi-million dollar facility, complete with an indoor swimming pool and gymnasium, that state officials in Columbus point to as a model for the state and country.

Mental health professionals and other educational groups constantly are dropping by the school to look over the program and talk to Seta. Though he believes this recognition from fellow professionals is the best kind, Seta and the school have received various awards. Seta received a citation for service to the handicapped from the President's Committee on Employment of the Handicapped in 1965 and the outstanding educator's award from the Cincinnati Police Department in 1969. The school unit received a special letter of commendation from the president of the National Association for Mental Health in 1972.

When people complain about conditions at Longview, hospital officials counter with a tour of the children's facility. The difference between the new unit, which just opened this fall, and the oldest section of Longview is about a century--in physical appearance as well as atmosphere.

"But the children's school unit has always been different," says Seta, protesting the comparison. "It has had community support." Other people say it has had Nick Seta.

What has caused Nick Seta to stay with the state mental hospital where it is commonly known that the pay is lousy, the hours long, the problems numerous and the possibilities for change strongly dependent on the whim of the legislature?

"I'm sort of addicted I guess," admits Seta. Leaning back in a comfortable chair in his office with some time to philosophize, he jokingly compares himself to Albert Schweitzer. "He could have written his own ticket, but where did he get his kicks? In the jungle.

"I deny the idea that people shouldn't get involved. Besides the word commitment, involvement is the best word." A person can go overboard, Seta concedes but admits a heavy dose of narcissism has saved him.

"The Bible says love thy neighbor as thyself. To me that means you've got to love yourself a hell of a lot before you can love somebody else."

Seta does not particularly blame the politicians for the conditions at Longview because "they only react to mandates thrown at them by the public and the public doesn't give a damn."

He recalled a television news team that received permission to film conditions at Longview and run it in five-minute segments, six straight nights. "Do you know what the response was?" he asks, suddenly getting excited. "One lousy letter asking why a television set on one of the wards was broken. It's the old out-of-sight-out-of-mind syndrome."

Ohio's prisons and mental institutions "are cesspools," according to Seta, because of a lack of real public interest. People are more interested in assessing blame than solving the problem, he says.

Can't something be done? Quoting from the historian Chesterton, Seta said, "Christianity didn't fail, it's never been tried."

He continues, "Until it happens to you or somebody in your family, you are not going to do anything about it." Unfortunately, state institutions don't attract men and women who can move their fellow man, Seta says, though good public relations departments and speakers bureaus would help.

The only thing Nick Seta believes would really move the public to action is personal involvement. "If every person in Cincinnati would take it upon himself to help one other person, we wouldn't need systems or institutions." But, getting back to reality, he said, "Don't look for that to happen."

Though Nick Seta's formal education includes a bachelor's degree in history and French, and a master's degree in education from Xavier University, he said he had no real contact with the mentally ill other than those "I grew up with."

"My own upbringing on the riverfront was the best education I could have had for this job," Seta says. "It was a rough environment in which you learned to survive."

Undoubtedly it has helped him relate to the problems of the juvenile delinquents and disturbed children whose lives he touches daily. "There is almost an instant instinctive relationship between us," he explains. "It is an open ballgame. I'm very primitive in my expressions and behavior. I think nothing of grabbing a kid and hugging him. I try to establish a relationship with each on a personal level."

The children in the school unit have disturbances ranging from severe psychosis to behavior problems. They are children from every socio-economic background, though in the past they were primarily from low-income areas. What causes their problems?

"It could be genetic, environmental, or a combination of both. Each factor plays a part , but who knows for sure. There are a lot of conflicting theories," he says. "I try not to play God. I can't do anything about the past."

The greatest obstacle to treating disturbed children, according to Seta, is that no one wants to take the blame. "Why assess blame?" Seta asks. "There's a problem to correct so let's get the job done."

Seta claims the term "emotional disorder" is relative, expecially in today's society. "Society says what is normal , but what society is accepting for normal behavior in the schools, I'd have gotten expelled for."

"A lot more kids today have emotional disorders," Seta says. "Look at the number of kids partaking in alcohol and drugs. It's out of sight."

"Don't take me wrong, I'm no doomsday guy," Seta cautions. "A lot of American kids are doing fine. But the biggest problem I see in society is the lack of discipline and I've been saying that since long before it became popular."

Society has made discipline synonymous with punishment when it is aimed at correcting behavior, Seta says. "We say do-your-own-thing to our kids , but they aren't ready for it. They are farther ahead intellectually than they are emotionally. It's self-destructive."

The job of the children's school unit is "to help the kids get their heads on straight--to resocialize them and re-educate them so they can live in society in a way they can be accepted," according to Seta.

"We do this through school, recreation, correct living environments and wholesome adult relationships," he explains. "But most important, we try to give these kids a healthy identification of who they are and some people they can hold on to."

"God knows we all need somebody to hang on to."

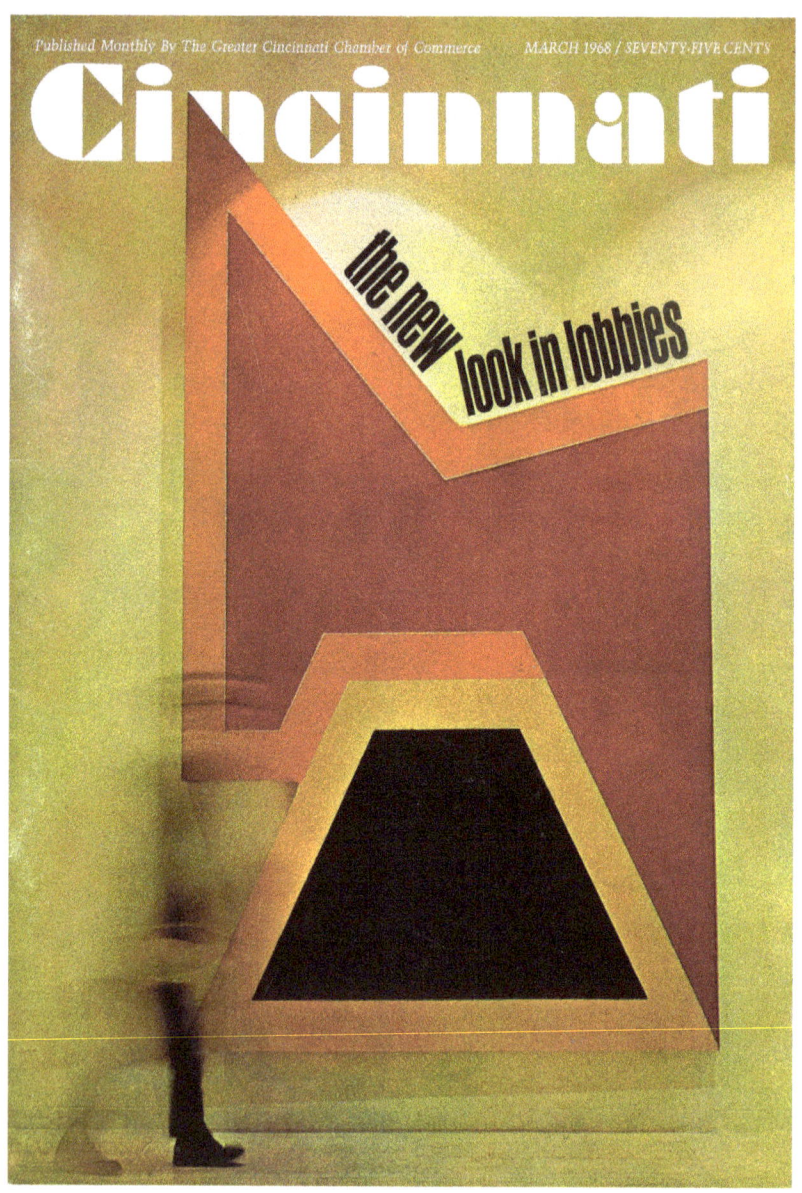

Cincinnati Magazine, March 1968

*The two sides of Nick Seta*

Reprint of Cincinnati Magazine Article, The Two Sides of Nick Seta

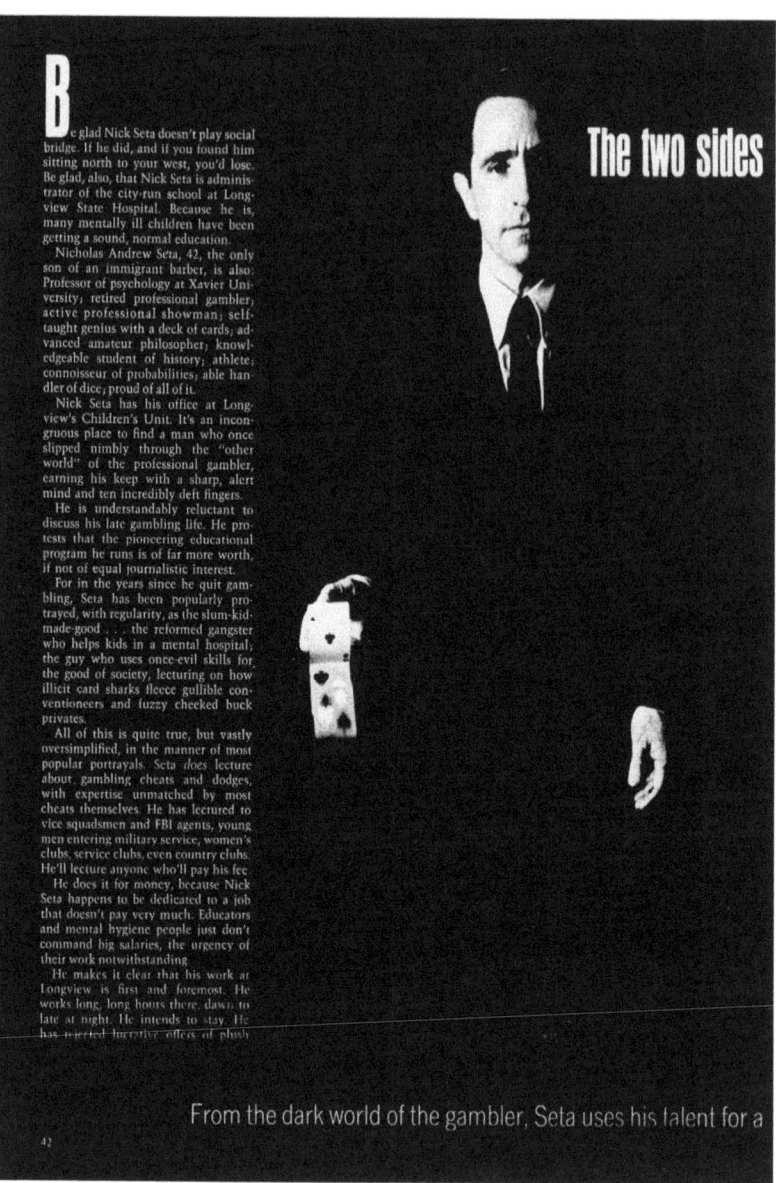

## The two sides

**B**e glad Nick Seta doesn't play social bridge. If he did, and if you found him sitting north to your west, you'd lose. Be glad, also, that Nick Seta is administrator of the city-run school at Longview State Hospital. Because he is, many mentally ill children have been getting a sound, normal education.

Nicholas Andrew Seta, 42, the only son of an immigrant barber, is also: Professor of psychology at Xavier University; retired professional gambler; active professional showman; self-taught genius with a deck of cards; advanced amateur philosopher; knowledgeable student of history; athlete; connoisseur of probabilities; able handler of dice; proud of all of it.

Nick Seta has his office at Longview's Children's Unit. It's an incongruous place to find a man who once slipped nimbly through the "other world" of the professional gambler, earning his keep with a sharp, alert mind and ten incredibly deft fingers.

He is understandably reluctant to discuss his late gambling life. He protests that the pioneering educational program he runs is of far more worth, if not of equal journalistic interest.

For in the years since he quit gambling, Seta has been popularly protrayed, with regularity, as the slum-kid-made-good . . . the reformed gangster who helps kids in a mental hospital; the guy who uses once-evil skills for the good of society, lecturing on how illicit card sharks fleece gullible conventioneers and fuzzy cheeked buck privates.

All of this is quite true, but vastly oversimplified, in the manner of most popular portrayals. Seta *does* lecture about gambling cheats and dodges, with expertise unmatched by most cheats themselves. He has lectured to vice squadsmen and FBI agents, young men entering military service, women's clubs, service clubs, even country clubs. He'll lecture anyone who'll pay his fee.

He does it for money, because Nick Seta happens to be dedicated to a job that doesn't pay very much. Educators and mental hygiene people just don't command big salaries, the urgency of their work notwithstanding.

He makes it clear that his work at Longview is first and foremost. He works long, long hours there, dawn to late at night. He intends to stay. He has rejected lucrative offers of plush

From the dark world of the gambler, Seta uses his talent for a

Reprint of Cincinnati Magazine Article, The Two Sides of Nick Seta

# of Nick Seta

public relations jobs where he could exploit his eloquence and cultivated salesmanship. He's just dedicated. Period.

Seta bears no malice when he refers to his salary. "If I had an axe to grind, I'd grind it," he says. Nick Seta is direct, forthright, and does not double-talk anyone. "I'm not looking for more dough." His life has reflected this.

He was born Dec. 18, 1925, in the southern Italian seacoast town of Fuscaldo. He keeps in his desk drawer, and eagerly displays, a picture postcard showing the house in which he was born. It was sent him by his parents, who went back to Italy when his father retired.

Nick was an only child. His parents emigrated to America when he was three. "Calabrians were often tailors and Cincinnati was a textile town. We were from Calabria. We came to Cincinnati."

Nick's father settled in Over-the-Rhine and for years ran a barber shop at Thirteenth and Main. Nick, like a lot of other Italian Catholic immigrant children, went to St. Mary School at Twelfth and Clay Streets.

He grew up in the Depression and shares with his contemporaries the singular pride of having lived to tell about it.

"There wasn't any question of bowling alleys or golf or swimming or cars. We played kick the can and football with a stuffed sock. I wouldn't trade it for anything," he says. Then he displays his acquired sophistication by discoursing on the downfall of Tennessee in the last minutes of the 1968 Orange Bowl.

Nick began experimenting with playing cards at 14, about the same time he entered Purcell High School. He found them fascinating. He explains his interest with unemotional logic, as if he were tracing the course of a river on a map. His city-streets neighborhood, with pool halls and saloons, and a depression atmosphere, gave kids little to shoot at in the way of heroes... except for the guys who could make a buck at cards, shoot pool for profit.

"A kid likes to play baseball, his goal is to make the major leagues. I liked to play cards, my goal was the big time," Seta says.

Being good at cards was something to shoot at. He shot. He hit.

rewarding adventure — helping emotionally disturbed children.

43

Reprint of Cincinnati Magazine Article, The Two Sides of Nick Seta

Nick was graduated from Purcell in 1943, a slender, dark-haired lad of 17, a record-holding athlete (track, boxing, baseball), and a budding "mechanic" with the instincts of a high-roller.

He went right into the Marines. By the time he reached the Pacific (Guam, the Marshalls, Okinawa) he had seen a lot of buddies relieved of a lot of payday cash by more or less professional card-players-in-uniform. He had relieved some of those buddies of cash himself. But his stern Catholic conscience started complaining somewhere down in the deck.

"So I rationalized. Instead of winning from my buddies in the Marines, I'd go over and win from the Navy guys instead. I started rationalizing everything I did as a gambler," he says.

He left the Marines at war's end, richer than he went in, slickly expert with cards. And he drifted into the professional's world.

"Now, you have got to realize, there are certain things I never tell. But to be as good as I am with a deck of cards, I didn't learn in the Boy Scouts. When I got out of the Marines, I messed around a lot on the West Coast. In San Diego, I'd go into bars and use the cards to win drinks for friends. The word got around. I was approached . . ."

Thus, with a quiet shrug, Nick Seta explains how he signed on as a pro.

What came next is vague, perhaps deliberately. He admits working his way, over an ill-defined period of a year or so, back to Cincinnati. He admits dealing for Jimmy Brink at Lookout House, and at the Latin Quarter in what once was Newport, Kentucky.

"There were some other places. Some were bust-out joints and some were legit. I'm not proud of dealing in dishonest games, but that's where the money was, Baby! A dealer in an honest game isn't anything. He gets maybe twenty a night. All he does is deal cards. Anyone could do it. But the dealer in the bust-out game really has got to know what he's doing. His life depends on it. And he gets a big salary and a percentage."

As he dealt his way back home, Seta found himself rationalizing more and more.

"I took a lot of dough off a guy in St. Louis once, playing gin. I remember rationalizing that by going to this church, Sacred Heart Church, and putting half the winnings in the poor box. You know, give God half, keep half for myself. I couldn't be all bad."

He also remembers "driving this big car and visualizing myself wrecking it because of how I got the money for it. I really worried about this. I got pretty neurotic over it."

Ultimately, he opted out for a college

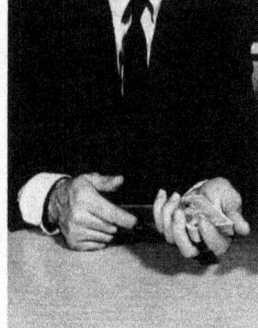

*The mechanical grip: tip-off to a crooked deal*

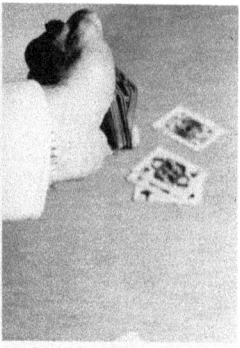

*Back-peeking: a glance at the top card*

career. To what extent gambling paid the tuition is unclear. Exactly when he retired as a pro is uncertain. That he majored in history at Xavier isn't.

"There was this priest I knew and admired. A fine, tough man. He was head of the history department so I majored in history."

He still quotes Toynbee, still draws analogies between contemporary America and Imperial Rome.

And somewhere along the line he got married. His wife, Roberta, is mother of his five children, ages 11 to 19. They hardly cropped up in our talk; they're his "private life," an entity he guards zealously and apparently regards as apart from his career. (The kids go to watch his gambling shows, but only when the occasion is suitable for children . . . "no booze, no broads," as he put it). The Seta family lives in contemporary American suburbia (Finneytown).

After graduation, Seta learned of a new education program for mentally ill children that a psychiatrist wanted to try out in a state hospital. He followed his acquired taste for the odds and decided to get in on the ground floor of something new and promising. So he went to work at Longview.

His ground-floor entry, and the success of his thoroughly straight forward, pragmatic approach to his work led him back to Xavier. When the college decided to create a course in the psychology of juvenile delinquency, Seta was called on to write the syllabus. He has since written three other courses for Xavier and seen them develop into the only masters degree program in the delinquency-psychology field. The courses are immensely popular, to the point of overcrowding.

At Longview, he now runs a school for 103 children (pre-school through high school) with two psychiatrists, two caseworkers, and eight teachers.

He runs it with stable good humor, nononsense, and arrow-straight administration.

The directness bends only a little in relaxed circumstances, and Seta is prone to digress. Even then, he makes cogent, discerning points with staccato frequency. His manner of speaking is hard to characterize. He can be softly fluent, firmly tough, quietly conspiratorial, profanely earthy . . . as the occasion demands. Five-dollar words mingle with pure slang.

"You know, Hollywood and TV always distort my worlds," Seta says. "People always get the wrong picture. The mentally ill person is always portrayed as one of those 5 per cent who are raving, frothing, hallucinating psychotics. It is not that way at all. There are degrees of psychosis, in a continuum.

"And they always portray the professional gambler as 'one of those dirty Mafiosi' who's mixed up in all sorts of vice like prostitution, dope, and who runs gambling joints so he can cheat people. But the real professional isn't that way. People get cheated because there just happens to be a lot of dishonest people around.

"The guy who runs a big legitimate casino in Las Vegas doesn't cheat. There are no absolutes; I'm not saying he doesn't have some connections somewhere. Hey . . . sure he has. And I'm not saying every casino is completely honest. But do they try to be completely honest. Ohh-h, you bet they do! They're dependent on it. They depend on their reputation.

"Someone's always trying to associate the Mafia with dishonest gambling. It isn't so. There are just a lot of dishonest individuals. The Mafia doesn't make the gambling crooked. Not if it can help it.

"Hell, they don't have to cheat. The way the game is built makes them win.

44

# Reprint of Cincinnati Magazine Article, The Two Sides of Nick Seta

164

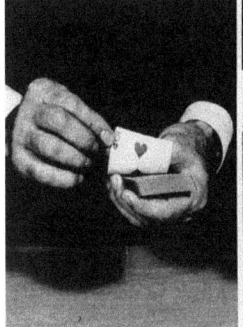 

Second dealing: the top card, a 3 of hearts ... but the king below is dealt

They set it right out there on the table for you. Like the crap table. There it is. You want to bet the big six or the big eight, they'll give you even money. And the odds are six-to-five against you. They can't lose. Why cheat?"

The cheats, the guys who fleece the gullibles, operate elsewhere, independently at conventions, on cruise ships, military bases, in the small bust-out games in the back room of a saloon. Let one set up shop in a big legit casino ... a Beverly Hills or a Lookout House of days past ... and the boss sees to it he's gone in a hurry.

"The world of professional gambling is vastly different from the supposedly upstanding middle-class world of legitimate business. In a way it's more honest. The professional gambler's world is black and white. There's none of this gray hypocrisy. The gambler's word is his bond. You make a deal and it's a deal. He won't promise to do business with you today and then be lured away tomorrow by someone with a more profitable proposition.

"And they don't have to keep their laws by killing everybody. If I welsh on a bet today, I don't get killed. But the word gets around. Tomorrow, when I go to make a bet, the book, he's got the word. He asks, 'Hey! You paid up with Johnny?' If I'm not, no transaction.

"But if I sell you a used car and con you good, you can talk all you want. But I can go next door tomorrow to make a deal and the guy there doesn't want to know anything but have I got the dough? He doesn't care that I cheated you, just so I don't do it to him."

The affluence of the professional gambling establishment is due largely to the sheer volume of business and the amazing pleasure with which people in a rich country pitch their money away.

"There's a thing we call the 'Ninny Variable'," Seta says. "A guy has a hundred bucks and he bets it. If he wins, he picks up and runs like hell. If he loses, he can't wait to run back to his room to get another hundred.

"When the pendulum swings his way, he's a chicken who bets small and runs away when he wins a little. But when the trend's against him, Oh Boy! He bucks it just as hard as he can. Boom! Boom!"

What Seta suggests ... if one must gamble ... is that one ride the winning streaks for all they're worth and learn to recognize the losing streaks so the loss can be minimized. He also feels most casino patrons are unaware of the simple fundamentals ... the mechanics of the game, the odds.

"There are thousands of people who sit down at a blackjack table and just sit and play. They don't think about odds. They don't watch the cards or count what's gone by. They just play and lose."

Seta's recreation runs to sports ... baseball, football, basketball, playing tennis, impromptu touch football with the college football players who work at Longview as part-time summer recreation aids. ("We play ten bucks a man to make it interesting. I can win. I'm just quick and nimble.")

Nick Seta does not play social cards. "I'm too dumb to play bridge. Professional gamblers do not play bridge. Oh, I could make sure our side got three of the aces, and let the rest fall at random, just to give us an edge. But my bidding'd kill us."

I asked: "Not even social poker?"

He replied: "What do you mean, 'social poker'? I won't play in a friendly game for two bits or a dime. I know the game too well. It's dull. If I'm going to play, it'll be worthwhile.

When he's not working, or lecturing, or with his family, Seta goes off, as he says, "to have a few drinks and watch a card game in a back room over the river, or just sit and talk to some of the people in the 'other worlds'. With a job like this, you have to just get completely away from everything once in a while or you go up the wall."

Then Seta moved on to what was supposed to be a demonstration of deceptive maneuvers with a deck of cards. It may have been deliberately fast ... after all, he is accustomed to a fee for demonstrating his skills. I wasn't paying.

But he reached into his desk drawer and pulled out the deck he keeps there all the time ("Just to amuse the kids, relax them, get them to talk over their problems."). He started riffling, cutting, shuffling, and flicking. It was so fast my eyes just gave up blinking and stared there, dripping tears. I kept one hand on my wallet, just in case.

The patter accompanying the display of virtuosity was as fast as the fingers. It went something like this: "This is the slickstack. And here's the flisterslip slide. Now for the glish ... watch. Or I can set you up with a move like this ..."

Move? What move?

"When I do my gambling shows, the extent of the show is whatever I feel the sophistication of the audience can tolerate."

I was flattered, I think.

Seta slowed down a bit and put the deck on the corner of his desk, face down. "Here's a new one I'm working on. Think of a card."

He picked the deck up and started fanning it out, still face down.

"Five of diamonds," I offered.

"There!" he said, as the five of diamonds appeared in the midst of the fan, the only one of the 52 that was face-up.

Again, with the nine of clubs. As he fanned them out, I watched his fingers. Not a trace of extraneous motion. But there was the club nine, staring up from a down deck.

And there was Nicholas Andrew Seta, multitalented wizard. He stooped with the lithe grace of an athlete and, in his fastidiousness, picked an infinitesimal dot of stray lint from the carpet. He sat down, behind his big desk.

There he was. Conservative blue pinstripe suit; fashionable, yellow tab-collar shirt; quietly bold blue and red print tie; black, grained laceless shoes. At eight in the evening, after a long, long day of demanding work in the underpaid world of the educator, he was neat, crisp, suave.

Not even a trace of five o'clock shadow.

Then it occurred to me! As we had sat there talking, he'd secretly lathered and shaved, showered, and changed to a clean shirt.

45

## Reprint of Cincinnati Magazine Article, The Two Sides of Nick Seta

165

# Nick's Expose on Gambling

### AN EXPOSE OF GAMBLING BY NICHOLAS A. SETA

Nick Seta, one time professional gambler now professional educator. Presently he is Director of the Childrens Unit at Longview Hospital and an Associate Professor at Xavier University.

His show is a demonstration aimed at giving us a glimpse into the mystic world of gambling . . During his performance he attempts to answer many of the questions related to this field by covering such areas as cards, dice, tops, logs, punchboards, etc. You will also get a close-up view of card-manipulations, such as: "Riffle-Location", "False-Cutting", "Rear-Peek", "Seconds", "One-Card Hold", and the "One-Hand Cut".

His primary purpose is to entertain us, but he also hopes a certain amount of education takes place.

Nick ready to do an Expose of Gambling

# The OASA REPORTER

NEWSLETTER OF THE OHIO ASSOCIATION OF SCHOOL ADMINISTRATORS — NOVEMBER, 1961

## THE ASSOCIATION

### The Case For Quality

For three years the annual OASA-OSBA convention has pointed up the need for improved educational quality in Ohio schools. This year is no exception. Under the theme "Ohio Can Provide Quality Education for All," the three-day conference, Nov. 14-16 at Veterans Memorial, Columbus, aims to show school board members, administrators and business officials how to more effectively use personnel, curriculum and financial resources in the quest for quality.

Highlight of the opening day program will be the 8 p.m. keynote address of Warren G. Hill, Maine commissioner of education. His address, aimed at lay and professional education leaders, is entitled "Uneasy Lies the Head That Wears A Crown."

Earlier, convention-goers will have an opportunity to see closed circuit television via Ohio State University's WOSU-TV, and a sample of a Midwest Airborne TV Project program on elementary science. MPATI President John E. Ivey, Jr., will host the 10 a.m. opening session.

**The Panel.** Tuesday afternoon the convention has scheduled a panel discussion on the ways to provide quality education. Chaired by Dorothy Fuldheim, Cleveland television news analyst, the group includes: State Senator Oliver Ocasek, Northfield; William Ware, assistant Sunday editor of the *Cleveland Plain Dealer;* W. E. Chope, president of Industrial Nucleonics, Columbus, and Forrest Moran, assistant superintendent, Newark.

Author Patricia Sexton will be a special consultant at one of the discussion sessions scheduled for Wednesday. A professor of education at New York University, Miss Sexton recently authored *Education and Income,* a study of the relationship of quality education to the family income.

Joining Professor Sexton in the group on "Evaluating Techniques for Quality Eduaction," will be Parma Supt. Paul Briggs. Chaired and planned largely by OASA members, the other nine discussion sessions include:

"Programs for Gifted Children" (Salem Supt. Paul Smith); "Winning Public Understanding and Support" (Leetonia Supt. Victor Wood); "School Ac-

Author Patricia Sexton
Education quality and income.

tivities in the Total Curriculum" (Exec. Head Edwin Greene, Sycamore); "The Architect's Contribution to Quality Education" (Newark Supt. Thomas Southard); "Job Descriptions" (Amherst Supt. W. A. Smith) and "Analyzing the Administrative Team" (Exec. Head Robert Lucas, Princeton).

On Wednesday evening, the convention will shift to the Deshler Hilton ballroom for a round-table conference on school financing. Aim of the discussion is a survey of member ideas on the methods OSBA can use to most effectively present school board views on finances to other state agencies.

While OSBA holds its Thursday morning business session, non-delegate board members will attend a series of clinics on specific school problems.

Registration will begin Tuesday morning at 9 a.m. in the Veterans Memorial Building. At the same time, exhibitors representing more than 200 firms will open their displays.

### That Man Again

For the first time in OASA history, there will be a repeat performance. Nicholas Seta, one of the most colorful personalities in U. S. education, will be on hand at the annual meeting Friday, Dec. 1, at the Deshler-Hilton at Columbus.

Five years ago, Seta held an overflow OASA annual meeting crowd spellbound, so much so that every administrator remained on hand until the last minute of the session.

Seta, ex-professional gambler and ex-Marine sergeant, who now plays a unique role in some highly-specialized phases of public education, will tell about his job as well as giving his fascinating demonstration of the tricks of crooked gambling.

Ex-Gambler Seta & Friends
A fascinating man, an unusual school job, an eye-popping show.

Page 1 OASA Newsletter, November 1961

167

# The OASA REPORTER

Published four times yearly by the Ohio Association of School Administrators, a department of the Ohio Education Association, 213 East Broad Street, Columbus 15, Ohio.

**EDITOR**
**ROBERT OLDS**

**Editorial Staff:** Marjorie Lauer, William E. Henry, Donald Schaub.
**Editorial Advisory Board:** W. E. Weagly, Erie County; W. A. Smith, Amherst.

## Ohio Association of School Administrators

**OFFICERS**

President .............. W. E. Weagly
Erie County
President-Elect ............ Carl Baden
Mariemont
Sec.-Treas. ............... W. A. Smith
Amherst

### COMMITTEES

**Executive Committee**—Dean O. Clark, Heidelberg College; Paul Gunnett, Springfield; Gordon Humbert, Canton; Harold Nichols, East Cleveland; Brooks A. Parsons, New Richmond; Thomas J. Quick, Franklin County; D. B. Roeder, Newcomerstown; John Shannon, Belmont County; Herschel D. West, Forest Hills (Hamilton).

**Legislative Planning Committee**—Thomas J. Quick, Franklin County, Chairman; Kermit L. Daugherty, Jackson, Vice Chairman; Carl H. Albrecht, Norwood; Ralph Ely, Barberton; Lee Grimsley, Portage County; E. W. Kavanagh, Greene County; Ralph McCambridge, Willard; H. C. McCord, Worthington; Allen Rupp, Marietta; C. Roland Swank, Elida (Allen); Ralph Tullis, Washington County; Harold A. White, Medina County; Victor C. Wood, Leetonia.

**Professional Relations Committee**—Paul Smith, Salem, Chairman; Paul Briggs, Parma; William Carter, U. of Cincinnati; L. G. DeLong, Ironton; Frank Dick, Sylvania; O. R. Edgington, Montgomery County; Sam Hicks, Ohio University; Ted Janson, Ohio State University; John Lea, Wayne County; Robert Lucas, Princeton (Hamilton); John Major, Solon (Cuyahoga); Chester Raush, Kettering; Roger Shaw, Kent State University; Robert W. Stanton, Kent; Robert Van Auken, Findlay; James Wooldridge, W. Clermont (Clermont); W. W. Zinser, Mansfield.

**Research Committee**—Hugh S. Morrison, Lucas County, Chairman; Marshall D. Boggs, Washington, C.H.; John Evans, Lorain; Alexander Frazier, Ohio State University; Roy D. McKinley, Coshocton; Richard Pheatt, Toledo; Harold Walker, Canton Local (Stark); J. H. Wanamaker, Youngstown.

**School Management Institute Directors**—Paul Gunnett, Springfield; Robert Lucas, Princeton (Hamilton); Ralph Mikesell, Eaton; Brooks Parsons, New Richmond; Wendell Pierce, Cincinnati; W. E. Weagly, Erie County.

OASA membership is open to superintendents, executive heads, professors of education and State Department of Education administrators. Send memberships ($5) to W. A. Smith, Sec.-Treas., 1260 Old Oak Dr., Amherst, Ohio. News contributions should be sent to: OASA Reporter, 213 East Broad St., Columbus 15, Ohio.

---

The meeting will be held starting at 11:45 a.m. Information about luncheon reservations will be sent to OASA members in advance of the meeting.

Another program feature will be the presentation of OASA's program of activities and services for 1962 by President-Elect Carl Baden, Mariemont.

The one-time dealer at the tables of Las Vegas and Reno will tell Ohio's top school administrators about his work in the Cincinnati school system as the education director of two highly specialized schools.

He directs one program for emotionally and mentally ill children at Longview State Hospital and another at the Juvenile Court Youth Center School. Both types of schools are unusual. The state hospital education program was the first to be instituted in the midwest and has been in operation 11 years. The juvenile court school is one of about a dozen of its kind in the nation.

He supervises a staff of 14 teachers plus recreation and other specialized workers in the two education programs.

Since his decision to expose the techniques of crooked gamblers, Seta has given more than 4,000 demonstrations. He holds an annual in-service course for the Cincinnati vice squad and lectures periodically to Ohio FBI agents. In addition to revealing mechanical gimmicks (for which Seta has great disdain), he shows how the hand can be quicker than the eye without the aid of artificial props.

**The Election.** Annual election of OASA officers also will take place. Proposed by a five-member nominating committee are the following for 1962 officers:

President — Carl Baden, Mariemont.
President-Elect — Robert Lucas, Princeton (Hamilton Co.)
Secretary-Treasurer — W. A. Smith, Amherst.
Executive Committee — Wendell Pierce, Cincinnati; C. A. Gibbons, Lorain Co.; Frank Dick, Sylvania, and Raymond G. Drage, Plain (Stark Co.).

Members of the nominating committee are: Paul G. Gunnett, Springfield, chairman; Ralph Ely, Barberton; H. C. McCord, Worthington; I. J. Nisonger, Boardman (Mahoning Co.), and W. A. Smith.

The OASA constitution provides that additional nominations can be made for any office in writing, signed by 50 or more active members, provided the additional nominations are sent to the Secretary at least 10 days prior to the annual meeting.

**25-Year Awards.** OASA members who meet requirements of administrative service as outlined in the 1961 OASA Directory, Page 31, will be presented the Association's Twenty-Five Year Award at the annual meeting. Members who believe they are eligible must send notification to Secretary Smith by Nov. 1.

**New Administrators.** Another annual meeting feature will be recognition of members who have joined the ranks of top school administration this year, serving for the first time as superintendents, assistant superintendents, administrative specialists or executive heads. President Weagly has asked that new administrators notify Secretary Smith by Nov. 1 inasmuch as state records may not be entirely complete.

## THE JOB

### Proposed Standards

New certification standards for top school administrators which have been proposed by the State Board of Education coincide generally with recommendations made by OASA through the Ohio Committee for the Advancement of School Administration. OASA President Weagly, President-Elect Baden and Past President Paul Gunnett all served on the Board committee which developed the State Board proposals.

The State Board is expected to take final action on the new standards at its December meeting, following a public hearing on Nov. 13. After adoption, the standards will become effective on January 1, 1963.

Proposed standards for executive heads and superintendents, however, omit two OCASA recommendations: (1) That candidates for provisional and professional executive head certificates and superintendent provisional certificates shall have an official recommendation from the college or university as well as completion of necessary training, (2) That agencies providing in-service education programs shall have Department of Education approval.

A grandfather clause will be included to protect the certification status of present administrators. According to Assistant State Supt. Harold J. Bowers, they will be able to continue to renew their present certificates under existing requirements. However, if they desire to raise their certification rank (i.e. provisional to professional) the new requirements will apply.

The new superintendent's provisional certificate calls for completion of 60 semester hours of graduate work in an approved institution with at least 10 semester hours completed "while in a period of continuous full-time resi-

THE HAND IS SLICKER — Nick Seta, center, demonstrates quick deals and fast shuffles as wives of Bellevue Chamber of Commerce members study the "action" at Thursday night's annual dinner meet. Left to right are Mrs. Robert Redd, Mrs. Ed Swartz, Seta, Mrs. Richard Raish and Mrs. Robert Harris.

The Bellevue Gazette, April 16, 1971

ANYONE FOR CARDS? — Nick Seta, center, director of Longview Children's Hospital, Cincinnati, talked about his past, as a professional card player at the annual Chamber of Commerce dinner Thursday night. Left to right are Phil Shaner, who introduced the speaker; Seta, and new chamber president Floyd Donahue.

Bellevue Chamber of Commerce Officers & Nick

## Home Front
### by Sandee

**THE WORST ADDICTION OF ALL**

Together with other persons working in either corrections or courts in Ohio, we learned all about cheating last Thursday evening. The "teacher" was Nick Seta, a multi-talented man. Seta is a professor at Xavier University and has been teaching psychology to those earning their Masters in Corrections. He also happens to be in charge of the Longview Hospital Children's Unit. Formerly, he was a professional gambler–a dealer in northern Kentucky whose talents helped him earn his way through college.

Seta was the speaker for the banquet of the Ohio Correctional and Court Services Association which had a two day conference last week at Xavier University and the Quality Motel Central in Norwood. Seta's remarks were important but brief. His demonstrations with cards and dice kept the audience enthralled for more than an hour.

The ex-gambler pointed out that we make much of alcohol or drug addiction but tend to negate the greatest addiction–gambling. He said that those addicted to gambling, and their families, are the most devastated people of all. He also commented that the establishment "is often in on it, adding, "if you place a bet with a bookie, you're a scoundrel; but if you bet at the racetrack, you're a sportsman".

If anyone in the audience believed that could spot a fixed game, before the demonstration, they certainly believed a lot differently after. Seta can tell you the stunt he is about to pull, then pull it, before your very eyes, and you just can't detect the action. He is not egotistical, but very much aware of his own talents which he uses now to spot cheating for law enforcement. He can easily convince you that you can't beat the odds created by the man who knows how to handle cards or who has special dice in a crap game. He displayed several dice that would fool the less sophisticated and a couple pair that could fool even an expert temporarily. In one pair, the difference could only be determined with a micrometer. Each die in another pair was heavier on one side because the paint weighed a fraction of an ounce more. The gambler could always determine the odds.

Seta can always know the card on the top of the deck, deal the second card without anyone knowing it wasn't the top card, stack any deck or have anyone pick a card and tell them which one of 52 it is. He never has to use a fixed deck and he doesn't care what kind of deck it is–old or new–he can manipulate it to his advantage.

Seta pointed out that some people are born with the talent for "cheating" just as others are born with a talent for art. Although he weighs only 138 pounds and is very short, his hands are far larger that those of a man six foot tall who weighs 170 pounds.

Courts and corrections people, especially those who have been in the field for a number of years, are not easily fooled. They have also "been around" enough to be a bit more suspicious than the average person. But I doubt if any of them came away from that session without a sureness that they, too, could lose their shirts if they got involved in a contest with a man like Seta.

The Professor feels it is a shame that when the public is warned about the professional gambler's tricks, as on TV, they are shown a skilled person rather than a talented one. Many viewers spot the trick and become convinced that they can spot any cheater; then, they get involved with real talent and figure that it's just their luck that's bad. In the process, they lose quite a bundle.

### Educator At Longview

# Former Gambler Is Speaker For Fort Hamilton Hospital Kick-off Dinner On Tuesday

Nicholas (Nick) Seta, administrator of the school at Longview State Hospital and professor of psychology at Xavier University, will speak at the Fort Hamilton Hospital Kick Off dinner Tuesday at 6 p.m. at Taft High School. Mr. Seta formerly was a professional gambler.

"Mr. Seta's experience as a teacher and administrator of the school at Longview provide him with interesting material to relate to an audience," said Frank Witt, general chairman of the Fort Hamilton Hospital Enrollment Campaign. Mr. Witt said he believes Mr. Seta will set the tempo for the forthcoming campaign.

A goal of 8,200 new and renewal memberships has been set for the campaign. More than 100 branches will participate in the enrollment drive. Supplies and information will be available at the meeting.

Money realized from the campaign is used for scholarships for young people who plan to enter nursing or hospital related careers.

The Harrison Flip Twisters under the direction of James Smith will entertain.

MR. SETA

www.ingramcontent.com/pod-product-compliance
Lightning Source LLC
Chambersburg PA
CBHW040732220426
43209CB00087B/1600